Policy Manual on Law, Policy and Sustainable Development

Research Outcome of First Edition of Nelson Mandela International Summer School on Law, Policy and Sustainable Development, 2021

D1825501

Policy Manual on Law, Policy and Sustainable Development

Research Outcome of First Edition of Nelson Mandela International Summer School on Law, Policy and Sustainable Development, 2021

Centre for Human Rights, University of Congo, DRC-Africa
Youth for Asia (Pan Asian Policy Organization)

Editor-in-Chief
Prof. Dr. Richard Lumbika Nlandu, Director, Centre for Human
Rights, University of Congo, DRC-Africa

Editors
Dr. Pascal Sundi Mbambi, Catholic University of the Congo (université catholique du Congo), DRC-Africa
Mr. Abhisekh Rodricks, University of Wroclaw, Poland

Associate Editor
Ms. Purnima Sharma, University of Wroclaw, Poland

CWP
Central West Publishing

This edition has been published by Central West Publishing, Australia
© 2023 Central West Publishing

For more information about the books published by Central West Publishing, please visit https://centralwestpublishing.com

Disclaimer
Every effort has been made by the publisher, editors and authors while preparing this book, however, no warranties are made regarding the accuracy and completeness of the content. The publisher, editors and authors disclaim without any limitation all warranties as well as any implied warranties about sales, along with fitness of the content for a particular purpose. Citation of any website and other information sources does not mean any endorsement from the publisher, editors and authors. For ascertaining the suitability of the contents contained herein for a particular lab or commercial use, consultation with the subject expert is needed. In addition, while using the information and methods contained herein, the practitioners and researchers need to be mindful for their own safety, along with the safety of others, including the professional parties and premises for whom they have professional responsibility. To the fullest extent of law, the publisher, editors and authors are not liable in all circumstances (special, incidental, and con-sequential) for any injury and/or damage to persons and property, along with any potential loss of profit and other commercial damages due to the use of any methods, products, guidelines, procedures con-tained in the material herein.

NATIONAL
LIBRARY
OF AUSTRALIA

A catalogue record for this book is available from the National Library of Australia

ISBN (print): 978-1-922617-32-3

Message from Jenny Leong MP
Member of the New South Wales Legislative Assembly, Australia representing the Greens

It is such a crucial time for you all to come together and forge a path ahead that puts human rights, social justice, sustainability and environmental protections as the top priorities.

After such a difficult period throughout the world, it is critical that we remain connected and work out ways forward for our planet that is based in a human rights approach with sustainability at its centre. An approach that seeks to address the inequality and injustice that exists - and that puts the interests of our local and global communities - and the good of our planet and future generations - at the heart of all decision making.

May your coming days be very productive and informative - and filled with new connections, new ideas and inspiration for how we can work together to address the many challenges we face.

Opening Address of the Summer University
(Professor Dr. Richard Lumbika, Director, Center for Human Rights, University of Congo, DRC-Africa)

This summer University opens in context where The Democratic Republic of Congo is facing a third stage of increasing of Covid-19 pandemic, provoking human rights restrictions. This pandemic, despite deplorable consequences, made us realize weakness of human being wherever he or she may be, equality of human and responsibility that he implies in universal level, the man's responsibility towards environment, humanity solidarity in preservation of environment, solidarity of present generation over future generations. International level of participants in this 3-day session reinforces the Conviction that Nations can no longer live individually or isolated, the responsibility of development, world's destiny and future generations are shared, albeit differentiated.

Dedicated to Nelson Mandela, I take this freedom to launch this summer University by an extract from his book « Conversation with myself », La Martinière, 2010, p.433: « Respect and even admiration are universal for those who are naturally humble and simple, and have an absolute faith in every human being, regardless their social condition

This is men and women known or not, that declares a total war against all forms of violation of human rights, wherever this excess take place in the world».

Thanks a lot to the organization, speakers and participants!

Good work!

Prof. Dr Richard Lumbika Nlandu, Director of CDH-UK
Editor-in-Chief

Editors' Note

The Policy Manual aims at establishing a linkage through various research papers as to the need for international cooperation on making policies for Sustainable Development Goals. The papers presented in this symposium have a common objective of establishing a broader networking among youth leaders and emancipators across the globe and bringing their ideas cumulatively to the table in a productive manner.

There lies an intuition among the authors of this policy manual and a vision which they truly believe in. They have identified the miniscule issues starting from grassroot level of policy formulation aiming to reduce existing social disparities and have extensively spoken about community level and global measures that can be adopted to tackle such problems and have given valuable suggestions as to how they think the problems at hand should be addressed. This manual consists of transnational issues of policy formulation and implementation of existing policies with greater effectiveness and provides statistical reasoning as to the ineffectiveness of the same.

Such a policy manual further aims to lay down comprehensive future plan and strategies that might empower the youth in order to make a significant transition in the world socio-political stage. The agenda to bring heads from all across the planet to discuss and take consideration of their views in regard to policy formulation and sustainable development of the planet is a great outcome of such a project itself.

This policy manual has briefly touched upon every aspect of human dignity and sustainable development in its entirety, starting from poverty upgradation to implementation of better educational facilities, even so as including the need of Artificial Intelligence in the policy framing domain, having talked about reproductive health of children and women and their rights, importance of entrepreneurship at grassroot community level, etc.

Finally, this manual lays down a clear-cut outline that the authors collectively envisage, towards bettering the global community and

complying to the SDGs, and the role of youth in collectively participating in policy formulation in their own individual capacity.

Dr. Pascal Sundi
Mr. Abhisekh Rodricks
Ms. Purnima Sharma

Acknowledgements

Rt. Hon. Dr. Kamal Sadat, PM - Minister of Information and Culture (Former), Deputy Minister of Youth Affairs, Islamic Emirate of Afghanistan

Hon'ble Mr. Justice Debangsu Basak - Judge, High Court, Calcutta, India

Prof. (Dr.) Nirmal Kanti Chakrabarti - Vice Chancellor, WBNUJS, India

Prof. (Dr.) Myrna Nisperos - Research Scientist and Resident Statistician, US Dept. of Agriculture, USA

Mr. Monruskin Calma - Director, Calma Expedition, Boston, USA

Prof. (Dr.) Wouter Vandenhole - Vice Dean (Research), University of Antwerp, Belgium

UNICEF Chair on Childrens' Rights (2013-2018)

Mr. John Buck, Founder – Governance Alive (International Governance Institute), Washington, USA

Prof. (Dr.) A.D.N. Bajpai - Vice Chancellor, Atal Bihari Vajpaye University, India

Dr. Ali Shameem - Former Chairperson – Maldives Civil Service Commission

Prof. (Dr.) Emmanuel Bueya, SJ - Hekima Institute of Peace Studies and International Relations (HIPSIR) – Nairobi/Kenya

Ms. Ajitha Menon - Political Economy Adviser, British Deputy High Commission (Kolkata), India

Ms. Paramita Neogi - Child Protection, Specialist, UNICEF, India

Mr. Thomson Chung - International Special Advisor, ASEAN Focus group, Co-Convenor-ASEAN-Australia Education Dialogue

Ms. Chiranthi Senanayke - Chevening Scholar, Birkbeck, University of London

Founder of HYPE, Sri-Lanka

Prof. (Dr.) Rathin Bandyopadhyay - Dean - Faculty of Arts, Commerce and Law, University of North Bengal, India

Ms. Bithi Roy - Field Officer, United Nations High Commissioner for Refugees (UNHCR), Bangladesh

Mr. Mahdy Hassan - National Program Officer, United Nations, Office on Drugs and Crime (UNODC)

Dr. Eddy M. - Political Scientist, Strasburg France

Contents

WOMEN'S REPRESENTATION AND FREEDOM THROUGH POLITICS IN BRAZIL

Thaiana Almeida Zandona

INTRODUCTION

PURPOSE

The purpose of this policy paper is to discuss the importance around the affirmation of women when it comes to politics and its representation around the public sector. It is directly interferes on how not only women are perceived as today, but also their quality of life and the reinforcement of longing standing social bias

Women and men are equal. Inherited to the same human rights. However, the affirmation on paper is vastly different from the daily basis occurrences where women, from the moment they are born, it is entitled a social gender bias that indistinctly nominated women as fragile, lesser than men and an ordeal of gender crimes ranging from sexual abuse to unequal payment. This plague that seems to constantly assist the structures of oppression, it is an undeniable factor that prevents society from achieving justice. This can be easily perceived in the occupation of women in congress seats. While most developing countries have democracy established, it is still a great challenge for women's legislative representation.

In Brazil, women are more than 50% of the citizen population, however our participation is very limited by social and structural beliefs in which not even the 30% of the obligated percentage it is met. This heavily translates to almost to non-gender-political discussion in any stage of the congress (city, state or country), constant rates of gender violence (more than 500 thousand notifications of sexual abuse per year) and denial of humanitarian rights for girls and women. An urgent analysis and a serious action-based in this situation as global participants, country and individual citizen.

CURRENT SITUATION

Minorities' representation in politics is a plural subject that requires a long-standing approach and a special consideration to culture, his-

1

tory and development of each country in the world. However, to maximize our approach and the extent of this work, the main point of this paper will be Latina America, focusing in Brazil, with some global highlights for reference.

It is crucial to understand this current situation. We intrinsically look to the current state and its social reflections but also integrated with a background perceptiveness to reflect on the situation. While all the countries in Latina America have amplified participation of women in politics, direct or not, especially in the last two decades after the re-democratization, the indices on representation show the challenge these countries may face to actual gender equality.

In November, 2020 after Brazil municipal elections, it was set a record on women's representation from Mayors to City Congress, including between the most voted trans-woman like Duda Salabert in the state of Minas Gerais. However as promising as the situation may appear there is a long way to go for women representatives for politics in Brazil and Latina America. For example, Brazil is in between election's policies reformulation that can deliberately work in favor of corruption and act against the minorities representation in congress. And this effect will already happen in the 2022 National Elections. Another two great threats to women in politics are gender-political violence and the popular called "orange candidates" where women are used in false applications.

On the same intensity that these women rise, there is a strong religion-based patriarchy they have to swim against. Not long distance from the disturbed 2020, Marielle Franco, a deputy from Rio Janeiro was brutally murdered after leaving an event that reunited black women from favela to talk about representation in 2016. Marielle was persecuted for being a lesbian woman acting against political corruption in Rio de Janeiro. Her case rests without a judgment with a direct criminal link to the President Bolsonaro's family. The impunity against this violence only reflects the real state of politics for women.

Women still have almost little to none voice representation and the political gender-violence is a constant threat as recently deputy Isa Penna from São Paulo was sexually harassed by a fellow male deputy in the middle of a parliament reunion.

Even more than 90 years after Brazilians sweetly conquered women's rights to vote, the way to congress is paved with violence, prejudice and lack of opportunities. Brazil has less women parliamentarians than Afghanistan. This is directly reflected on all women's lives in Brazil. Not one minute goes by without a violence being committed against them. Gender-based violence is a rotten culture, but the longing standing of no punishment is the reflection of our politics and public policy, or better, the lack of it.

BACKGROUND

To understand the situation on women's rights and political participation it is necessary to look back at the history in multiple points that peak at today's display. While it will present a general discussion on Latina America and Brazil's History, it is crucial to know this region is multiple and diverse. Not all perspectives apply equally to all countries.

Proceeding on this whole picture, this Region's background is shaped by, firstly, its colonization pattern to which slavery, native erasement, exploration and culture determination were used to form an identity that later will be directly connected to how women are perceived as individuals. After this section of exploration, Latin America, especially Brazil, were left in a very poor economic state, an enormous gap to real democratization and civil participation which associated with the previous identity and culture replacement, created prejudices that are withheld until today. This is easily seen through 20th civil wars, military intervention and the re-democratization process that happened all over America.

The women's condition at this culmination of history is translated as inadequacy of human's rights. In other words, for a very long time, women were not seen as individuals outside patriarch institutions.

According to the statement, direct examples:

- o Hyper-sexualization of Latina woman;
- o Structured race against black Latina women, especially their placement as servant;
- o Wipe-out of non-Christian religions and cultural backgrounds, leading to a patriarchal system, demonization of

other cultures, discrimination against native women and objectification of matriarchal structures.

If it is easy to simply reserve mandatory places for women in elections, the response to why those women do not get elected or even go through this process, is because we have developed a culture that interpreted women as not part, or not qualified enough, to participate in such process and eventually bring women's demands to political discussions.

THE IMPORTANCE

When we look at scenarios as the one mentioned before it is crucial to understand why women's political representation matters. Women's participation in politics, policy making and civil activism is a gain to the true meaning of democracy. There is strong evidence that as more women are elected to office, there is also a corollary increase in policy making that emphasizes quality of life and reflects the priorities of families, women, and ethnic and racial minorities. Women's political participation has profound positive and democratic impacts on communities, legislatures, political parties, and citizen's lives, and helps democracy deliver.[1]

The way women work can also be a factor to analyze the situation. Women tend to be more open to discussions, less vertical hierarchy with a more team-constructive approach which can often lead to work across party lines.

Research shows that women lawmakers tend to see "women's" issues more broadly as social issues, possibly as a result of the role that women have traditionally played as mothers and caregivers in their communities,[2] and that more women see government as a tool to help serve underrepresented or minority groups.[3]

---

[1] National Democratic Institute for International Affair - Handout 1 "Why Women in Politics?"

[2] O'Connor, K. (Undated) "Do Women in Local, State, and National Legislative Bodies Matter?" The Women and Politics Institute, American University.

4

Evidence from developing countries around the world shows that an increase in women's participation in the political life of their countries often leads to improved socio-economic conditions, as many of these women-- more readily than their male counterparts-- tackle poverty reduction and service delivery as areas of primary importance to their constituents and supporters, as can be seen in Rwanda.[4]

Another important feature in women's participation through law-making is regarding armed conflicts and peace building. Women are generally more affected by wars and conflicts and they tend to advocate more often for peace conflicts. Including women in the early stages is including half of the population, it is to bring representation and democracy to longstanding the agreements.

Research and case studies suggest that peace agreements, post-conflict reconstruction and governance have a better chance of long-term success when women are involved.[5]

Women as political leaders also prioritize education, health and development. Fourteen percent of women legislators in the U.S. named healthcare as a top priority issue, versus only six percent of male

---

[http://www.oklahomawomensnetwork.com/doc/Why%20Women%20Matter%20paper.doc].

[3] Camissa, A. and B. Reingold (2004) "Women in State Legislators and State Legislative Research: Beyond Sameness and Difference" in *State Politics and Policy Quarterly*. Vol. 4, No. 2: 181-210.

[4] Wilber, Roxane (2011) "Lessons from Rwanda: How Women Transform Governance." *Solutions*. http://www.thesolutionsjournal.com/node/887.

[5] Chinkin, C. (2003) "Peace Agreements as a Means for Promoting Gender Equality and Ensuring the Participation of Women." United Nations: Division for the Advancement of Women. [http://www.un.org/womenwatch/daw/egm/peace2003/reports/BPChinkin.PDF].

legislators who viewed health care as a top concern.[6] Using data from 19 OECD countries, researchers found that an increase in women legislators results in an increase in total educational expenditure.[7]

A research conducted directly for this policy paper, shows that 100% of the participants considered Women's participation in Politics to be "utterly important". It is a truth that when women are part of democracy, citizens tend to feel more represented and have more confidence in politics.

Kofi Annan noted, "Study after study has taught us, there is no tool for development more effective than the empowerment of women. No other policy is as likely to raise economic productivity or to reduce child and maternal mortality. No other policy is as sure to improve nutrition and promote health, including the prevention of HIV/AIDS. No other policy is as powerful in increasing the chances of education for the next generation."[8]

FUTURE PUBLIC POLICIES ACTIONS

To foster representation and reinforce democracy, evident-based actions are necessary. And when we look at scenarios such as the one presented throughout this paper, it is evident that public government participation needs to occur. However, when this come-across point happens it is automatic the rise of conflict, especially in countries such as Brazil where the polarization summed with very violent expressions can lead to the same circle trap of inequality and minimal real discussion and change being seen.

---

[6] Center for American Women and Politics (CAWP) (1991) "The impact of women in public office: findings at a glance." Eagleton Institute of Politics, Rutgers – The State University of New Jersey.

[7] Chen, Li-Ju (2008) "Female Policymaker and Educational Expenditure: Cross- Country Evidence." Research Papers in Economics 2008: 1 Stockholm University, department of Economics, revised, Feb 27, 2008. [http://ideas.repec.org/p/hhs/sunrpe/2008_0001.html].

[8] Moccia, P. (ed) et. al. (2007) *The State of the World's Children - 2007*. UNICEF. [http://www.unicef.org/sowc07/docs/sowc07.pdf].-

Point in mind, we cannot be detained by this. As much as this is real, the fear of confrontation cannot be a factor to not generate public policy proposals around women's political representation.

The Law sanctioned in September 30, 1997 obligated electoral parties to hold at least 30% of their candidates' vacancies for women. However only in 2012 this minimum began to be met. And even after it, when most political parties were colligations during the elections, they simply covered their numbers with one another, so in practical action they were not meeting the criteria. Only in 2019 this type of practice was stopped by the Supreme Federal Tribunal. This same court also decided that 30% of the Election Fund should be directed to women.

However, recently two very contradiction laws are being discussed. One of them, already approved by the Senates, is amnesty to parties that do not meet the 30%. In other words, if they don't compromise with the 30%, nothing actually happens. Another controversial discussion is the obligated but progressional occupation of 30% seats by women in Congress. While it may appear very honorable for the mandatory seats, the progressional part puts Brazil behind most countries by 20 years. This, because the actual 30% will only happen in 2038 as the percentage progresses - it will start with 18% for 2022. Both of these proposals show the inadequacy of public policy when it comes to women's participation.

One of the first policies to be issued is the punishment to political parties that do not meet the 30% criteria and/or try to cover their real numbers with collusions and justifications such as "orange candidates". The process of holding parties countable benefits the manufacture of democracy, reassuring that all citizens are being represented. This not only shows disrespect to women, but also works against the utterly disturbing levels of corruption in Brazil's Democracy as The Corruption Perception Index 2020 illustrates where Brazil's score 38 out 100 and it occupies the 98th place out of 180.

Another implementation should establish itself in the educational sector where there is a direct conversation with the culture around the topic. The lack of representation doesn't happen only in the congress and political department, but it solidifies the base through education.

All the participants in this research form, mentioned educational programs to be a way to combat the underrepresentation. For example programs which address the history of women in politics, especially the positive aspects of this participation. Or political education itself that is severely under looked in Brazil's system. Approaching this subject on an early learning stage offers the possibility to change the culture and views around the theme. To the young girls this will demonstrate representation and encouragement. To young boys, women in politics and their necessary respect will set off as normalcy. To those non-binary or trans it also possibilities their representation and a sense of democracy security as mentioned in "The Importance" when women are in political leadership positions the citizens feel more confident.

To conclude this approach to public policy, there is one standing factor which is the lethal effect to democracy: The political gender violence. This deeply rotten culture uproots all the work towards women in politics. There is no space for them if there isn't a guarantee of their human and constitutional rights as citizens. This type of violence occurs from inside their houses, to the political parties, internet and public spaces. From defamation, to constantly mansplaining, menterruption, gaslighting, to physical abuse. Women in politics are being dismissed, discouraged and mistreated. As a democracy, Brazil should, with the utmost urgency, secure women's interests and participation in political areas.

There is no discussion that to successfully obtain results from policy making and assure the rise in representation, it is essential a policy to punish and address this violence. One must follow these women trajectories to identify any possible threat and misconduct, to offer a secure place to reporting and do not victimize these women, but rather charge the true miscreants.

CONCLUSION

To close this research, I would like to reinstate, if isn't already perceived, the courage of women in politics throughout the whole world, but with an honorable mention to Brazil. As much as the benefits of women in politics are outnumbered, the violence, culture and underrepresentation they have to face is tearing. It incites us as a society to continually look for new research development and assume our responsibilities in standing against gender inequality.

This paper concludes the inevitable role of the public sector, lawmaking policy and the State in delivering justice, rights and accountability. Daring to say, the government needs to assume its own responsibility and problematic figure in this system. More than laws and discussions, it needs to take place the real debate and implementation of public policies to assure women's rightful participation in politics as well as their voices heard and stories told.

To Brazil, there is not only need in policy but also the patriarchal culture that it's now present at our highest power, like President Bolsonaro who constantly undermines discourse prejudice, religion-hatred and criminal speeches against women.

If we have hope in a sustainable development through gender equality and women in political spheres, this has to start by who we elect as our representatives and later as our lawmakers. Further, as Madeleine Albright has stated, the world is wasting a precious resource in the dramatic underrepresentation of women in leadership positions, often resulting in the exclusion of women's talents and skills in political life.

THE SNAG OF POLICY OF SEXUAL AND REPRODUCTIVE HEALTH AND RIGHTS

Tanaya Das
Chanakya National Law University

ABSTRACT

Sexual and reproductive health and rights (SRHR) have gradually been recognized in the international and national arena, but their evolution and the definition of their scope and content have been fraught with challenges and controversies. Elements of sexual and reproductive health and rights have always been a part of the human experience, but it was not until the mid- to late-1970s these terms were used and defined by major international organizations. Numerous reasons exist for the lack of recognition of sexual health and for its lack of adequate prioritization worldwide. It was always subsumed as reproductive health and was usually defined narrowly as the absence of sexually transmitted infections (STIs). Such associations reflect the way that the intersection of health with sex and sexuality is often portrayed in popular media and public health programs as dangerous and problematic, due to this discomfort with sex and sexuality, and the connected stigma, has even plagued the scientific study of the subject. From population control to human rights, from demographers' competence to governmental prerogative, from couples' rights to universal rights, these are the stages through which SRHR evolved over time.

Defining sexual and reproductive health is complex because it cuts across traditional measurement lines. While the exact etymologies of the phrases: reproductive health, reproductive rights, sexual health, and sexual rights are not clear as it encompasses not only physical, emotional, psychological dimensions but also social, ethical, moral, cultural and spiritual concerns.

There has long been an intimate connection between social policy and the study of sexuality. The realization of sexual health has been recognized as integral part of the 2030 Sustainable Development Goals (SDGs) relating to health, education, and gender equality. The social and developmental consequences of sexual and reproductive decisions are often further reaching than the health consequences. SDGs also call for provisioning of reproductive health services into national strategies and programmes.

Although there have been many progresses at international and national arena but efforts to implement these policy changes have been slow and fraught with obstacles from the effects of decentralization, a lack of resources, gender inequities and a reluctance to acknowledge youth sexual activity. The pandemic has revealed how health landscape is shaped by growing global, regional, national and local interdependence, in which all countries are challenged by major social, economic, environmental and demographic shifts. Significant inequalities in health remain, and in many places are worsening. Furthermore, health policy-makers often lack the authority and tools to lead a coherent, integrated approach to these important challenges.

This policy paper is divided into four parts: Part I discusses about the evolution of SRHR, past trends of their evolution and conditions under which changes occurred. Part II discusses about the definition of the terms related to SRHR. This part also explores, this failure to address or include issues of sexual health is a consequence of conservative power in a diverse set of social and political institutions. Part III discusses about the intersectionality between SRHR and development and its interconnections with diverse thematic areas of human rights. This part also explores the gaps and compliance of SRHR components in India, Congo and Brazil. Part IV examines the need for pre-legislative consultation or public engagement affords the benefit of legitimacy to laws arrived at through citizen participation as it informs decision-makers of the lived experiences of those most likely impacted by the legislation. Laws that receive pre-legislative consultation are attuned to realities, which increases the likelihood of their effectiveness. Times when human rights focused have increased on the sexual rights of women and of LGBTQ populations, as well as on other aspects of sexual health, the need for more comprehensive, systematic, and applicable definitions of sexual health and rights has grown call for political and public health leadership from the communities itself. This part will also analysis the need for Comprehensive Education on Sexuality (CES) for promotion, recognition and enforcement of SRHR.

Introduction

April 7th 2021 was 73rd anniversary of Health Day and the theme for this year's health day was: *Building a fairer and healthier world for everyone* ("World Health Day 2021: Building a fairer, healthier world for everyone", 2021).[9] As the world is undergoing through pandemic it is an opportunity to pause and reflect on challenges related to health and their responses. On the one hand, human rights in health have become institutionalized with an array of norms and standards and professionalized with vital roles in key global and national institutions, and on the other, the global health paradigms seem to have become increasingly dislocated from the movements that inspired the global recognition of health as a human right.[10]

The identification of what is wrong must come from those who are experiencing those wrongs.[11] People working on the evidence agenda such as academics, think tank researchers, experts in official statistics must work in correspondence to social movements.[12] The health and human rights movement, policies and frameworks have failed on this point.[13]

---

[9] *World Health Day 2021: Building a fairer, healthier world for everyone.* Eu-patient.eu. (2021). Retrieved 8 September 2021, from https://www.eu-patient.eu/news/latest-epf-news/2021/world-health-day-2021-building-a-fairer-healthier-world-for-everyone/#:~:text=To%20build%20a%20healthier%2C%20fairer,after%20the%20COVID%2D19%20crisis.&text=Awareness%20about%20Duchenne%20is%20the%20power!.

[10] *WMA - The World Medical Association-Right to Health.* Wma.net. (2021). Retrieved 21 October 2021, fromhttps://www.wma.net/what-we-do/human-rights/right-to-health/#:~:text=The%201948%20Universal%20Declaration%20of,%E2%80%9C1.

[11] Khosla, R. (2020). Health and human rights at crossroads. Health and Human Rights Journal, 22(1), 336 Article PMID: 32669813

[12] Ruth Levine. (2019, April 24) Closing the Gap Between Social Movements and Policy Change. Hewlett Org. Retrieved September 08, 2021, from https://hewlett.org/closing-the-gap-between-social-movements-and-policy-change/

[13] Khosla, R. (2020). Health and human rights at crossroads. Health and Human Rights Journal, 22(1), 335-338 Article PMID: 32669813

Sexual health and its elements on its own is rarely discussed in the halls of the United Nations or of organizations working on global health and it is generally, subsumed as reproductive health Whenever mentioned, it is most often linked to sexually transmitted infections (STIs).[14] Therefore, such negative associations reflect the way the intersection of health with sex and sexuality is often portrayed in popular media and public health programs: *as dangerous and problematic.*[15] This discomfort with sex and sexuality, and the concomitant stigma, has plagued even the scientific research of the subject. It is only from last few decades that the topic of sexual health, has received appropriate attention and consideration.[16]

Evolution Of SRHR And Trends Related to It

While SRHR has increasingly been recognized and defined in the international arena, this evolution and recognition is fraught with controversy. The development of these rights cannot be read in isolation but needs to be analyzed as part of the wider social and political movements, ideologies, and religions.[17]

Before 1994, SRHR were viewed as domain of demographers. The World Population Conference in 1954 in Rome and 1965 in Belgrade discussed issues of population growth and manner in which it can be controlled. SRHR were not conceptualized in terms of human rights but were viewed as the domain of demographers. The idea

---

[14] Wellings K, Cleland J (2001). Surveys on Sexual Health: Recent Developments and Future Directions. Article sti.77.4.238. http://dx.doi.org/10.1136/sti.77.4.238

[15] Starrs, A. M., & Anderson, R. (2016). Definitions and debates: Sexual health and sexual rights. Brown Journal of World Affairs, 22(2), 7-24

[16] Starrs, A. M., & Anderson, R. (2016). Definitions and debates: Sexual health and sexual rights. Brown Journal of World Affairs, 22(2), 7-24

[17] Orford, A. (2012). In Praise of Description. Leiden Journal of International Law, *25*(3), 609-625. http://doi:10.1017/S0922156512000301

which prevailed was: *World population is increasing at an alarming rate and this would lead to danger to mass starvation.*[18]

In the Bucharest World Conference on Population 1974 the discussion was on the issue of population growth and its relation to development. At this conference World Population Plan of Action (WPPA) was also adopted which recognized that population policies should be consistent with human rights and demanded that States should respect and ensure these rights regardless of their demographic goals.[19] It also recognized the right to decide freely and responsibly on the number and spacing of children and role of women in population policies.[20] However, the major failures were: instrumentalization of women's bodies to achieve population goals women's specific reproductive responsibility disregarded gender equality.[21]

It was not until late 1970s the elements of SRHR were defined by WHO and became part of human rights.[22] Generally, it is agreed that the concept of SRHR has emerged from the women's health movement in the 1960s and from institutions such as WHO in the 1980s and 1990s.[23] These movements lead to the conference of 1994.

---

[18] Kellogg, Alfr. (1970). Population Growth and International Law. Cornell International Law Journal 3: 93-100. Article 7. http://scholarship.law.cornell.edu/cilj/vol3/iss1/7
Retrieved September 08, 2021, from
[19] United Nations Population Division. (1974a). UN World Population Conference. 1974. World Population Plan of Action (WPPA). Bucharest. E/CONF, 60/L. 55. New York: United Nations Population Division.
[20] United Nations Population Division. (1974a). UN World Population Conference. 1974. World Population Plan of Action (WPPA). Bucharest. E/CONF, 60/L. 55. New York: United Nations Population Division.
[21] Cook, Rebecca J., Bernard M. Dickens, and Mahmoud F. Fathalla. (2011). Reproductive Health and Human Rights: Integrating Medicine, Ethics, and Law. Oxford Scholarship Press. http://1093/acprof:oso/9780199241323.001.0001
[22] Starrs, A. M., & Anderson, R. (2016). Definitions and debates: Sexual health and sexual rights. Brown Journal of World Affairs, 22(2), 7-24.
[23] Starrs, A. M., & Anderson, R. (2016). Definitions and debates: Sexual health and sexual rights. Brown Journal of World Affairs, 22(2), 7-24.

The International Conference on Population and Development (ICPD) in Cairo 1994 became decisive moment in the international discussions on population as it brought a major shift in the thinking and approach to population of issues-from pure population control through family planning to a much wider aspect.[24] The discourse transformed from population control to a more comprehensive and positive approach of sexuality and reproduction which should be free from coercion, discrimination, and violence.[25]

ICPD brought SRHR in positive light and enhanced its development as the policies related to SRHR were built on the cornerstones of human rights. However, it also represented an important compromise on a topic of abortion,[26] which was treated not as a means of fertility regulation or as a legitimate reproductive health service but as something that must be prevented.[27]

An important effort towards achieving SRHR was adoption of Millennium Development Goals (MDGs). One of those goals (MDG 5) related to improvement in maternal health and called for a 75% reduction in maternal mortality ratios from 1990 levels by 2015.[28] At the 2005 World Summit, MDGs were expanded, and signatory governments committed to work toward universal access to reproduc-

---

[24] Pizzarossa, L. (2018). Here to stay: The Evolution of Sexual and Reproductive Health and Rights in International Human Rights Law. Laws, 7(3), 1-17. https://doi.org/10.3390/laws7030029

[25] Pizzarossa, L. (2018). Here to stay: The Evolution of Sexual and Reproductive Health and Rights in International Human Rights Law. Laws, 7(3), 1-17. https://doi.org/10.3390/laws7030029

[26] Pizzarossa, L. (2018). Here to stay: The Evolution of Sexual and Reproductive Health and Rights in International Human Rights Law. Laws, 7(3), 1-17. https://doi.org/10.3390/laws7030029

[27] Berer, Marge. (2009). The Cairo "compromise" on Abortion and Its Consequences for Making Abortion Safe and Legal. Reproductive Health and Human Rights: The Way Forward. Philadelphia: University of Pennsylvania Press, pp. 152-163.

[28] Yamin, A., & Falb, K. L. (2012). Counting What We Know; Knowing What to Count. Nordic Journal of Human Rights, 30(3), 350-371.

tive and sexual health care by 2015[29] and another target MDG 5B relating to universal access to reproductive health, was added.[30] However, MDGs failed to address the importance of SRHR in improving health and in promoting economic and gender empowerment and just focusing on maternal health rather than on sexuality and reproduction was considered detrimental to achievement of human rights as they are indivisible in nature.

Upon the success of the expired (MDGs) in 2015, members of UN adopted the 2030 Agenda for Sustainable Development a universal agenda comprising the Sustainable Development Goals (SDGs), a framework of 17 goals and 169 targets for the period 2015 to 2030.[31] Issues of SRHR were recognized from onset of SDGs. Goals specifically related to SRHR:

A. Goal 3: Ensure healthy lives and promote wellbeing for all at all ages.[32] This goal lays down the target of universal access to sexual and reproductive healthcare services, including family planning, information and education, and the integration of reproductive health into national strategies and programmes.[33]

---

[29] Goicolea, I., San Sebastian, M., & Wulff, M. (2008). Women's Reproductive Rights In The Amazon Basin Of Ecuador: Challenges For Transforming Policy Into Practice. Health and Human Rights, 10(2), 91-104.

[30] Yamin, A., & Falb, K. L. (2012). Counting What We Know; Knowing What to Count. Nordic Journal of Human Rights, 30(3), 350-371.

[31] UN General Assembly. (2015) Transforming Our World: The 2030 Agenda for Sustainable Development, A/RES/70/1. Retrieved September 09, 2021, from https://www.refworld.org/docid/57b6e3e44.html

[32] UN General Assembly. (2015) Transforming Our World: The 2030 Agenda for Sustainable Development, A/RES/70/1. Retrieved September 09, 2021, from https://www.refworld.org/docid/57b6e3e44.html

[33] UN General Assembly. (2015) Transforming Our World: The 2030 Agenda for Sustainable Development, A/RES/70/1. Retrieved September 09, 2021, from https://www.refworld.org/docid/57b6e3e44.html

B. Goal 5: Achieve gender equality and empower all women and girls.[34] This goal can only be achieved when females have bodily autonomy which can be ensured when harmful practices such as child and forced marriage and female genital mutilation are eliminated.[35]

However, SDGs like MDGs adopted limited scope of SRHR. It failed to recognized Sexual Rights in general and Safe Abortion Care, Sexual Orientation and Gender Identity were not discussed and mentioned.[36] The failure on part of international organization to address SRHR comprehensively and progressively is a consequence of conservative power in a diverse set of social and political institutions as recognizing it would amount to accepting sexual behavior outside traditional set practices and change social, cultural and institutional practices.[37]

The Intersectionality Between SRHR And Development.

SRHR is multidimensional as it operates on individual, relational, familial, and community levels as well as in multiple realms-

---

[34] UN General Assembly. (2015) Transforming Our World: The 2030 Agenda for Sustainable Development, A/RES/70/1. Retrieved September 09, 2021, from https://www.refworld.org/docid/57b6e3e44.html

[35] UN General Assembly. (2015) Transforming Our World: The 2030 Agenda for Sustainable Development, A/RES/70/1. Retrieved September 09, 2021, from https://www.refworld.org/docid/57b6e3e44.html

[36] IPPF: Africa Region. SDG's and SRHR: What's in it for SRHR?
https://www.google.com/url?sa=t&rct=j&q=&esrc=s&source=web&cd=&cad=rja&uact=8&ved=2ahUKEwibiM2oqvjyAhVCXSsKHR1_BNoQFnoECAIQAQ&url=https%3A%2F%2Fwww.ippfar.org%2Fsites%2Fippfar%2Ffiles%2F2017-01%2FSDG%2520E%2520fn.pdf&usg=AOvVaw0UmsXgq_sOn6pHvz5ZbZ1d

[37] UN Committee on Economic, Social and Cultural Rights (CESCR). (2000) General Comment No. 14: The Right to the Highest Attainable Standard of Health (Art. 12 of the Covenant), E/C.12/2000/4, Retrieved September 10, 2021, from https://www.refworld.org/docid/4538838d0.html

psychological, physical, social, and political.[38] Sexual and reproductive health is a state of complete physical, mental as well as social well-being in all matters relating to sexuality and the reproductive system.[39] Definition of sexual and reproductive health given by UNFPA states that it implies that people are able to have a satisfying and safe sex life, the capability to reproduce, and the freedom to decide if, when, and how often to do so.[40]

The comprehensive definition of SRHR was proposed by the Guttmacher–Lancet Commission which covers sexual health, sexual rights, reproductive health and reproductive rights.[41] The definition reflects on evolving consensus on the services and interventions needed to address the sexual and reproductive health needs of all individuals.[42] Also, it addresses issues of violence, stigma and respect for bodily autonomy, which profoundly affect individuals' psychological, emotional and social well-being. Further, SRHR of neglected groups is specifically addressed by it. Therefore, SRHR is an

---

[38] Starrs, A. M., & Anderson, R. (2016). Definitions and debates: Sexual health and sexual rights. Brown Journal of World Affairs, 22(2), 7-24.

[39] United Nations Population Fund. (2019). Sexual And Reproductive Health and Rights: An Essential Element of Universal Health Coverage Background Document For The Nairobi Summit on ICPD25: Accelerating The Promise.
Retrieved September 10, 2021 from https://www.unfpa.org/sexual-reproductive-health#readmore-expand

[40] United Nations Population Fund. (2019). Sexual And Reproductive Health and Rights: An Essential Element of Universal Health Coverage Background Document for The Nairobi Summit on ICPD25: Accelerating the Promise.
Retrieved September 10, 2021 from https://www.unfpa.org/sexual-reproductive-health#readmore-expand

[41] Starrs, Ann, and others (2018). Accelerate progress – Sexual and Reproductive Health and Rights for All: Report Of The Guttmacher–Lancet Commission. Lancet, vol. 391, pp. 1642–92
doi: http://10.1016/S0140-6736(18)30293-9.

[42] Starrs, Ann, and others (2018). Accelerate progress – Sexual and Reproductive Health and Rights For All: Report Of The Guttmacher–Lancet Commission. Lancet, vol. 391, pp. 1642–92
doi: http://10.1016/S0140-6736(18)30293-9.

extensive term that covers a range of issues. It includes not only sexual behavior and reproductive capacity but also sexual identity, gender identity, sexual orientation, roles, personality, relationship patterns, thoughts, feelings, attitudes, bodily and reproductive autonomy.[43] It encompasses not only physical, emotional, psychological dimensions but also social, ethical, moral, cultural and spiritual concerns.[44]

The fact cannot be denied that SRHR is essential element for good health and development be it economically, socially or individually. Without taking under consideration population's SRHR needs, Universal Health Coverage (UHC) is impossible to accomplish, as many of the basic health needs are connected to people's sexual and reproductive health.[45] Poor sexual and reproductive health interventions and outcomes is one of the leading factors for global burden of death and disease for the ages between 15 to 44 years, with unsafe sex a major risk factor for death and disability in low- and middle-income countries.[46]

---

[43] TARSHI. (2018). Sexuality And Disability: in the Indian Context Retrieved September 10, 2021 from https://www.tarshi.net/inplainspeak/tarshis-corner-working-paper-sexuality-and-disability-in-the-indian-context-2018/

[44] TARSHI. (2018). Sexuality And Disability: in the Indian Context Retrieved September 10, 2021 from https://www.tarshi.net/inplainspeak/tarshis-corner-working-paper-sexuality-and-disability-in-the-indian-context-2018/

[45] United Nations Population Fund. (2019). Sexual And Reproductive Health and Rights: An Essential Element of Universal Health Coverage Background Document for The Nairobi Summit on ICPD25: Accelerating the Promise.
Retrieved September 10, 2021 from https://www.unfpa.org/sexual-reproductive-health#readmore-expand

[46] World Health Organization (2014) Women and Health: 20 Years of the Beijing Declaration and Platform for Action. Executive Board EB136/18, 136th session.
Retrieved September 10, 2021 from http://apps.who.int/gb/ebwha/pdf_files/EB136/B136_18-en.pdf

Adoption of SDGs led to the commitment of achieving UHC along with financial risk protection, access to high-quality essential health-care services and access to safe, effective, high-quality and affordable essential medicines and vaccines for all.[47] Prevention of maternal and newborn deaths could be possible by improved access to well-integrated reproductive health services, together with ante-natal care, skilled attendance during childbirth and immediately af-ter birth, and emergency obstetric care for complications.[48] Improv-ing sexual and reproductive health is the most cost-effective of all development investments, reaping personal, social and economic benefits. It will save and improve lives, slow the spread of HIV and AIDS, prevention of early and unwanted pregnancies, encourage gender equality. It will help to stabilize population growth and re-duce poverty. Reducing high fertility can create opportunities for economic advancement if the right kinds of social policies there in action.[49]

The Gaps and Compliance of SRHR Components

Globally, people living in low- and middle-income countries experi-ence higher levels of morbidity and mortality attributed to sexual and reproductive health due to high rates of population growth, poor health infrastructure and lack of scientific and unbiased infor-

---

[47] United Nations Population Fund. (2019). Sexual And Reproductive Health and Rights: An Essential Element of Universal Health Coverage Background Document for The Nairobi Summit on ICPD25: Accelerating the Promise.
Retrieved September 10, 2021 from https://www.unfpa.org/sexual-reproductive-health#readmore-expand
[48] Department for International Development. (2004). Sexual and reproductive health and rights: A position paper
Retrieved September 10, 2021 from http://gsdrc.org/document-library/sexual-and-reproductive-health-and-rights-a-position-paper/
[49] Department for International Development. (2004). Sexual and reproductive health and rights: A position paper
Retrieved September 11, 2021 from http://gsdrc.org/document-library/sexual-and-reproductive-health-and-rights-a-position-paper/

mation which is a pre-condition for making informed choices and decisions.[50]

On global scale, MDG 5 was successful but the policies framed were parochial in nature and inappropriate indicators were adopted to measure national progress.[51] SRHR, which is not simply the absence of maternal mortality.[52] Gradually, there has been progress in recognition of sexuality, sexual orientation and gender identity. This progress can be analyzed with help of policies of few countries.

India

Abortion is a crime for both the woman and the doctor, except to save the woman's life.[53] Thus, it is still an exception. Although the recent amendment act has extended the upper gestation limit from 20 to 24 weeks for women falling under special category which includes survivor of rape, victims of incest and in cases of substantial fetal abnormalities there is no gestational limit but it has failed to recognized the need for safe abortion and reproductive health services.[54]

---

[50] World Health Organization. (2010). Social Determinants of Sexual and Reproductive Health: Informing Future Research and Programme Implementation
Retrieved September 11, 2021 from
https://www.who.int/reproductivehealth/publications/social_science/9789241599528/en/
[51] Yamin, A., & Falb, K. L. (2012). Counting what we know; knowing what to count. Nordic Journal of Human Rights, 30(3), 350-371.
[52] Yamin, A., & Falb, K. L. (2012). Counting what we know; knowing what to count. Nordic Journal of Human Rights, 30(3), 350-371.
[53] Hirve S.S (2004) Abortion Law, Policy and Services in India: A Critical Review, Reproductive Health Matters, 12:sup24, 114-121.
https://doi.org/10.1016/S0968-8080(04)24017-4
[54] Hirve S.S (2004) Abortion Law, Policy and Services in India: A Critical Review, Reproductive Health Matters, 12:sup24, 114-121.
https://doi.org/10.1016/S0968-8080(04)24017-4

Despite the fact that one-third of the population is young they don't have access to sexual and reproductive health services sue to over-burdened health sector and highly conservative practices and policies.[55]

In recent years the Supreme Court has given judgements related to gender equality and autonomy. Right to privacy was recognized as fundamental right in Puttaswamy judgement.[56] In Joseph Shine, the court struck down Section 497 of the IPC and decriminalized adultery.[57] In Navtej Johar the Supreme Court of India struck down part of Section 377 of the Indian Penal Code that criminalized same-sex relationships between consenting adults.[58]

Brazil

From last few decades there was expansion and universalization of Brazil's public policies for education and health.[59] But international Catholic movement, along with other pro-life groups, negated all the progress made in the field of SRHR in last five years (2014-1018) and laid the foundations of conservative moral guidelines.[60]

---

[55] National Human Rights Commission & SAMA Resource Group for Women and Health. (2018). Status Of Human Rights in The Context of SEXUAL HEALTH AND REPRODUCTIVE HEALTH RIGHTS IN INDIA
http://www.samawomenshealth.in/srhr-country-assessment-report/   ;
https://dx.doi.org/10.2139/ssrn.3348988
[56] *Justice K S Puttaswamy (Retd.), & Anr V. Union of India And Ors.* (2017) 10 SCC 1
[57] *Joseph Shine V. Union of India* (2018) SCC OnLine SC 1676
[58] Navtej Singh Johar v. Union of India AIR 2018 SC 4321
[59] Brandão R. Elaine & Silva Cabral C. al (2019) Sexual and reproductive rights under attack: the advance of political and moral conservatism in Brazil, Sexual and Reproductive Health Matters, 27(2), 76-86
https://doi.org/10.1080/26410397.2019.1669338
[60] Brandão R. Elaine & Silva Cabral C. al (2019) Sexual and Reproductive Rights Under Attack: The Advance of Political And Moral Conservatism in Brazil, Sexual and Reproductive Health Matters, 27:2, 76-86
https://doi.org/10.1080/26410397.2019.1669338

22

A number of legislative initiatives intended to veto the expansion of abortion rights and overturn the legalization of free abortions in public health services network.[61] Another series of policy initiatives aimed at destabilizing the achievements in the civil and political rights of the LGBTQ population and tried to exclude any content related to gender and sexuality from being taught in the country's public schools and universities.[62]

Congo

In Africa, the debate regarding sexual orientation and gender identity is acrimonious due to strong opposition from socially conservative cultural and religious traditions.[63] Sexual and reproductive rights are some of the most controversial, underdeveloped, and least understood spheres of rights, especially in Africa.[64] The major portion of population in the continent is of youths and majority of them are sexually active from the age of 17. Also, adolescent pregnancy and childbearing at young age is high. The risk of dying from an un-

Rosenberg A. The Brazilian Paradox: The Lesbian, Gay, Bisexual, and Transgender Battle for Human Rights, Topical Research Digest: Revisiting Human Rights in Latin America, 16-30

[61] Diniz G. S. & Araújo J. M. (2015) Commentary: Reproductive health and rights in Brazil 20 years post-International Conference on Population and Development, Global Public Health, 10(2), 183–185
http://dx.doi.org/10.1080/17441692.2014.986167

[62] Brandão R. Elaine & Silva Cabral C. al (2019) Sexual and reproductive rights under attack: the advance of political and moral conservatism in Brazil, Sexual and Reproductive Health Matters, 27(2), 76-86
https://doi.org/10.1080/26410397.2019.1669338

[63] Kuwali, D. (2014). Battle for sex: Protecting sexual(ity) rights in africa. Human Rights Quarterly, 36(1), 22-60.
https://www.jstor.org/stable/24518096

[64] Murungi, L., & Durojaye, E. (2015). The Sexual and Reproductive Health Rights of Women with Disabilities in Africa: Linkages between the CRPD and the African Women's Protcol. African Disability Rights Yearbook, 3, 3-30.

safe abortion is exceptionally high in Africa countries.[65] Africa has the worst SRHR indicators and the largest youth population.[66] Democratic Republic of Congo (DRC) ranks 8th among top ten countries with the greatest number of women aged 20–24 who gave birth by age 18.[67] The region has high adolescent fertility rate which can be attributed to low levels of education especially among girls; the low status of women, few alternative economic opportunities; cultural norms that encourage large families.[68] From past few years there has been steady increase in programmatic initiatives to address adolescent and young people's sexual and reproductive health.[69]

[65] World Health Organization. (2010). Social Determinants of Sexual and Reproductive Health: Informing Future Research and Programme Implementation
Retrieved September 11, 2021 from
https://www.who.int/reproductivehealth/publications/social_science/97 89241599528/en/
[66] IPPF: Africa Region. SDG's and SRHR: What's in it for SRHR?
https://www.google.com/url?sa=t&rct=j&q=&esrc=s&source=web&cd=&c ad=rja&uact=8&ved=2ahUKEwibiM2oqvjyAhVCXSsKHR1_BNoQFnoECAIQ AQ&url=https%3A%2F%2Fwww.ippfar.org%2Fsites%2Fippfar%2Ffiles% 2F2017-01%2FSDG%2520E%2520fn.pdf&usg=AOvVaw0UmsXgq_sOn6pHvz5ZbZ1 d
[67] Mulumeoderhwa M. (2016). A Girl Who Gets Pregnant or Spends the Night With A Man Is No Longer A Girl: Forced Marriage In The Eastern Democratic Republic of Congo. Sexuality & Culture.20(4):1042–62.
[68] Romaniuk A. Persistence of high fertility in tropical Africa: the case of the Democratic Republic of the Congo. Popular Development Review 2011;37(1):1-28.
http://10.1111/j.1728-4457.2011.00388.x.
[69] Muanda F., Gahungu P., Wood F. & Bertrand J. (2018). Attitudes toward sexual and reproductive health among adolescents and young people in urban and rural DR Congo, Reproductive Health, 15(74)
https://doi.org/10.1186/s12978-018-0517-4

Pre-Legislative Consultation & Comprehensive Education on Sexuality (CES)

The identification of what is wrong must come from those who are experiencing those wrongs.[70] The lack of such public consultation and communities' participation in legislative formulation has led to several poorly drafted laws which have failed address needs and interests of affects groups.[71] This process involves holding consultations with interested groups and persons on the proposed policy, before a bill is drafted.[72] Thus, effectiveness and legitimacy of laws and policies.[73] Incorporating consultation and deliberation ensures that the law or policy comprises the broadest range of interests and is in accordance with public priorities and values, which furthers the goals of legalism.[74]

However, the process of pre-legislative in Sexual and reproductive health policies is only possible when communities have scientific and unbiased information around sexual health is a pre-condition for making informed sexual choices.[75] People have different and

---

[70] Khosla, R. (2020). Health and human rights at crossroads. Health and Human Rights Journal, 22(1), 335-338.

[71] Jain D. (2019). Law-Making by and for the People: A Case for Pre-legislative Processes in India, Statute Law Review, 20(20) 1-18. http://10.1093/slr/hmz005

[72] Jain D. (2019). Law-Making by and for the People: A Case for Pre-legislative Processes in India, Statute Law Review, 20(20) 1-18. http://10.1093/slr/hmz005

[73] Jain D. (2019). Law-Making by and for the People: A Case for Pre-legislative Processes in India, Statute Law Review, 20(20) 1-18. http://10.1093/slr/hmz005

[74] Karpowitz C. et al. (2009) Deliberative Democracy and Inequality: Two Cheers for Enclave Deliberation among the Disempowered 37 Politics and Society 576-615. http://doi.org/10.1177/0032329209349226

[75] United Nations Population Fund. (2019). Sexual And Reproductive Health and Rights: An Essential Element of Universal Health Coverage Background Document For The Nairobi Summit on ICPD25: Accelerating The Promise.
Retrieved September 12, 2021 from https://www.unfpa.org/sexual-reproductive-health#readmore-expand

changing sexual and reproductive health needs throughout their lives.[76] Thus, these different stages require access to different sets of SRHR interventions and the way in which these rights and needs are realized, at one stage in life has implications for sexual and reproductive health outcomes and needs during other stages of life. This can be achieved by applying a life course approach when implementing essential sexual and reproductive health and rights interventions. Age-appropriate and evidence-based Comprehensive Sexuality Education (CSE) is one of the essential methods of life course approach to lead to better sexual and reproductive health.

The excuses related to cultural norms and traditional practices are not valid excuse for not providing people with CSE that they need in order to lead a dignified and healthy life.[77] Enjoyment of the right to sexual education plays a crucial preventive role and may be a question of life or death.

Recognizing threat of HIV/AIDS and SITs, especially for groups at risk and persons in particularly vulnerable situations, such as women and girls exposed to gender-based violence or persons in difficult financial circumstances, transgenders, sex workers and adolescents CSE is extremely important.[78] However, restricting sexual education to the issue of SITs gives a limited view of sexuality and this may create an erroneous association between sexuality and disease.[79]

[76] United Nations Population Fund. (2019). Sexual And Reproductive Health and Rights: An Essential Element of Universal Health Coverage Background Document for The Nairobi Summit on ICPD25: Accelerating the Promise.
Retrieved September 12, 2021 from https://www.unfpa.org/sexual-reproductive-health#readmore-expand

[77] UN General Assembly. (2010). Report of the United Nations Special Rapporteur on the Right to Education. A/65/162 Retrieved September 12, 2021 from https://digitallibrary.un.org/record/688657?ln=en

[78] UN General Assembly. (2010). Report of the United Nations Special Rapporteur on the Right to Education. A/65/162 Retrieved September 12, 2021 from https://digitallibrary.un.org/record/688657?ln=en

[79] UN General Assembly. (2010). Report of the United Nations Special Rapporteur on the Right to Education. A/65/162 Retrieved September 12, 2021 from https://digitallibrary.un.org/record/688657?ln=en

CSE should include scientifically accurate, realistic, non-judgmental information.[80]

The right to education includes the right to sexual education, which is both a human right in itself and an indispensable means of realizing other human rights, such as the right to health, right to health, the right to information.[81] Even UN treaty bodies have also observed that the lack of access to sexual and reproductive education as a barrier to compliance with the State's obligation to guarantee the rights to life, health, non-discrimination, education and information.[82]

Conclusion

Sexual orientation, gender, gender expression, and sexual activity are historically, culturally, religiously, legally, and socially complex. Thus, achieving SRHR comprehensively is not an easy task. The outbreak of pandemic has shown how fragile the health infrastructures are and what adverse impacts the world can face if the health issues are not addressed intersectionality and multidimensionally. The pandemic has also exposed and intensified inequalities within and among countries.[83]

---

[80] United Nations Educational, Scientific and Cultural Organization (UNESCO). (2009). International Guidelines on Sexuality Education: Evidence Informed Approach To Effective Sex, Relationships And HIV/STI Education ED-2009/WS/36 Retrieved September 12, 2021 from https://www.refworld.org/docid/4a69b8902.html
[81] International Council on Human Rights Policy. (2009). Sexuality and Human Rights, Discussion Paper
Retrieved   September   12,   2021   from
https://reliefweb.int/report/world/sexuality-and-human-rights-discussion-paper
[82] United Nations Educational, Scientific and Cultural Organization (UNESCO). (2009). International Guidelines on Sexuality Education: Evidence Informed Approach To Effective Sex, Relationships And HIV/STI Education ED-2009/WS/36
Retrieved   September   12,   2021   from
https://www.refworld.org/docid/4a69b8902.html
[83] United Nations. (2021). The Sustainable Development Goals Report 2021

Previous public health emergencies have shown that the impact of an epidemic on sexual and reproductive health often goes unrecognized, because the effects are generally the indirect consequences of strained health.[84] Additionally, responses to epidemics and public health emergencies further exacerbate gender-based and other health disparities.[85] The marginalized communities such as LGBTQ and disabled people face triple discrimination in these responses. Countries' effective and evidence-based decisions to prioritize SRHR interventions hinge on a solid understanding of the existing SRHR needs within their population.[86] Every country is in different position in terms of resources, capacity, policy and legal environment. The preliminary step would be to adopt comprehensive definition of SRHR and then to progressively realize this approach through a step-by-step expansion of provided interventions. Taking stepwise approach in this manner would ensure optimum utilization of re-

---

Retrieved September 13, 2021 from
https://unstats.un.org/sdgs/report/2021/

[84] Riley T., Sully E., Ahmed Z. & Biddlecom A. (2020) Estimates of the Potential Impact of the COVID-19 Pandemic on Sexual and Reproductive Health In Low- and Middle-Income Countries, International Perspectives on Sexual and Reproductive Health, 46, 73 – 76
https://www.guttmacher.org/journals/ipsrh/2020/04/estimates-potential-impact-covid-19-pandemic-sexual-and-reproductive-health

[85] Riley T., Sully E., Ahmed Z. & Biddlecom A. (2020) Estimates of the Potential Impact of the COVID-19 Pandemic on Sexual and Reproductive Health In Low- and Middle-Income Countries, International Perspectives on Sexual and Reproductive Health, 46, 73 – 76
https://www.guttmacher.org/journals/ipsrh/2020/04/estimates-potential-impact-covid-19-pandemic-sexual-and-reproductive-health

[86] United Nations Population Fund. (2019). Sexual And Reproductive Health and Rights: An Essential Element of Universal Health Coverage Background Document for The Nairobi Summit on ICPD25: Accelerating the Promise.
Retrieved September 12, 2021 from https://www.unfpa.org/sexual-reproductive-health#readmore-expand

sources, effective multilateral development, improved lifestyle and realization of human rights.

CHILD RIGHTS AND ACCESS TO THE JUSTICE IN INDIA DURING THE COVID-19 PANDEMIC

Nabeela Tareen Khan
Central University of Kashmir, India

INTRODUCTION

Human beings by virtue of being humans are granted certain fundamental rights, such rights are referred to as human rights. Children are also independent humans and thus are entitled to the same human rights as any other person. A universally accepted definition of "child" includes 'a person who is below the age of eighteen'[87].

All children undergo a special stage of growth and overall development; thus, it becomes imperative that the special needs of the children are catered to. Children, on account of their developing minds and bodies, are often more vulnerable to abuse and exploitation. It is a common notion to perceive children as a property of the parents or guardians, their opinions, decisions and desires are not valued and additionally, they have no say in the important decisions of their life. Such prevalent conduct makes it necessary that some special rights are made to protect the children. These special rights are called the child rights. These rights are designed keeping in view ensured protection, nourishment and empowerment of children to their best capacities irrespective of their gender, class, creed, ethnicity, race etc. These rights have arisen out of a special need to progress the overall welfare of children. These Rights are fundamental, interdependent and inalienable in nature.

The Convention of the Rights of Children 1989 is an international treaty designed for the protection and promotion of child rights. It is a comprehensive document dealing with a range of rights which are civil, culture, religious and economic and so on

---

[87] Article 1, Convention of the Rights of Children (Signed on 20-November,1989)   Retrieved   on   1-August-2021   from   :
https://www.ohchr.org/en/professionalinterest/pages/crc.aspx

THE COVID-19 PANDEMIC AND ITS IMPACT ON THE RIGHTS OF CHILDREN.

The year 2019 is marked as the birth of the Covid-19 virus which has affected the entire world population across the globe. Covid-19 has generated an unprecedented pandemic worldwide. The crisis seems to have crippled the world economically, socially, in respect to health and has resulted into a humanitarian crisis, forcing people to be locked inside their homes. Children have undergone a multi-faceted impact and due to their vulnerable nature, they have been exposed to a high risk of violation of their rights. The pandemic has pushed the children to various abuses ranging from sexual, psycho-logical, physical and maltreatment. The United Nation's policy brief[88] expresses concern that the Covid pandemic has profoundly impacted the children. The impact is unevenly distributed among children from different countries, with children from the poorest of the countries being the worst hit.

The impact on the children is multi-dimensional. One of the major impacts is the disruption of the education of children all around the world. It has resulted into a learning crisis as schools have been closed down in almost 188 countries. Many countries have explored

---

[88] Policy report: The impact of Covid-19 on Children (Dated 15th April, 2020)

the alternative options of virtual learning but adopting this in low-income countries who lack basic amenities does not appear to be viable.

Poverty which is a global concern itself seems to worsen in the Covid Pandemic, especially in respect to children. As per the policy report, around 386 million children are undergoing absolute poverty as of 2019 and the number is likely to increase by 42-66 million (approx.). Some other abuses which have directly worsened the pandemic, includes lack of health care facilities, poor hygiene service resulting in death of children and increase in the infant mortality rates. Further, with the extended lock-downs, children are forced to live inside their house where they may be exposed to facing or witnessing abuse or violence children are more likely to be pushed into child marriage, prostitution, forced labour and overall to survive in extremely dire conditions to make ends meet. Especially children living in the conflict zones or undergoing refuge crisis, the Covid virus has further added to their mental and physical agony.

INDIA AND CHILD RIGHTS

India, who stands as a patriot of welfare society has a robust mechanism in respect to protection of children and their rights. The country offers a plethora of statutes ranging from specific laws dedicated to the protection of children to international undertaking and obligations. The Constitution of India which is the fundamental law of the land reflect child rights. Article 21A which is a fundamental right guarantee to compulsory and free education to all children between the age of 6-14. Further, Article 24 (a) makes available the right for children to be protected from hazardous employment and Article 23 ensures protection from trafficking and bonded labour. Art 14 which guarantees equal rights and equal protection before the laws is applicable on the children as well. Article 15 (3) empowers the state to make special laws for women and children. Apart from Constitutional rights, there are many statutes such as Indian Penal Code, Prevention of Children from Sexual Offences Act, 2012 which protect all children from all sexual offence listed in the act, Prohibition of Child Marriage Act, 2008 which makes marriage of a minor an offence, The Immoral Traffic (Prevention) Act, 1987 which protects children from trafficking, Child Labour (Prohibition and regulation) Act, 1986 etc. among others.

At an International level, India is an ardent advocate of child rights and has successfully ratified the United Nations Convention on the Rights of the Children in 1992. The efficiency of the laws depends critically on the implementation structure adopted. On account of that, India has attempted to introduce a micro approach when dealing with the child right protection. There is protection available from national to village level. However, the Covid-19 has severely exposed the dichotomy of the legal system in relation to access to justice for children.

The pandemic has resulted in over 1.2 Lakh children being orphaned, many of them compelled to take up unsafe migration, such children who are travelling on the roads are left with no food or livelihood, exposing them to abuse, assault, child marriage, and even adopting transactional sex as means to earn. Further, children belonging to the vulnerable communities are sharing an equal burden of suffering. For example, queer children are more likely to undergo abuse, witness mental trauma and forced treatments. Additionally, children of the sex workers and trans communities whose means of earning depends solely upon sex work and dancing are more prone to involve their young children into flesh trade to make up for their reduced income.

HOW FAR HAS THE COUNTRY BEEN SUCCESSFUL IN PROTECTION OF RIGHTS OF CHILDREN AND ENSURING UNHINDERED ACCESS TO JUSTICE (COVID- CONTEXT)?

The Government of India has to face a number of challenges in addition to tackling the Covid-19 Pandemic, the country is yet not in a position to shift its major functioning in the virtual space. Despite that, the country has adopted some responses to tackle the issue. The country has initiated various social protection measures (including setting up helpline centers), attempted to improve health care service including special attention to mental health. Access to Justice (e.g., Supreme Court Suo moto ordered direction for children affected due to Covid) and efforts have been made to ensure continued access to education and introduction to community-based learning, gender-based programs among others. However, the question that how far has the country been successful in the rights of the children being protected and that there is unhindered access to justice becomes imperative.

- A research study to analyse the question was undertook with 63.8% female, 34% male and 2.1% belonging the others category. 12.5 % of the participants were parents. The age group varied from 13- 50.

Figure 1: **Are you aware of the concept of Child rights?**

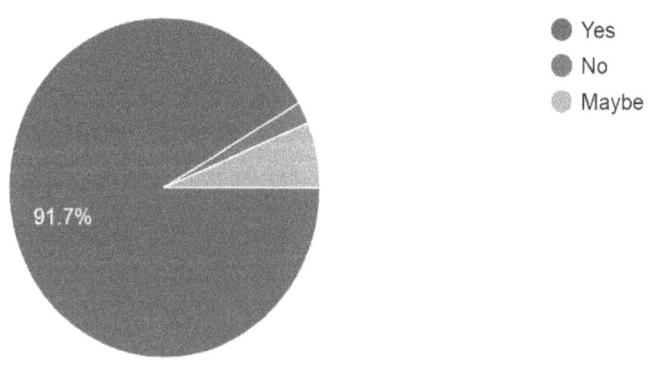

- It was found that 91.7% of the participant were aware of the concept of child rights. While 6.3% were somewhat aware of the idea and 2.1% of the participant responded negatively regarding the awareness of child rights.

Figure 2. **Do you think that the Covid19 lockdown measure/quarantine measure have impacted the children of India in terms of violation of their rights?**

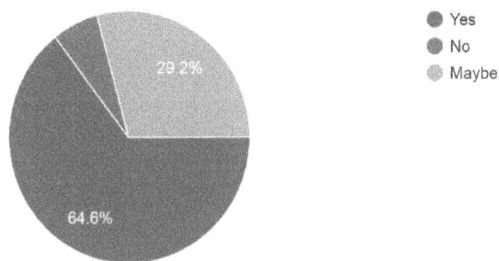

- When asked if they could agree that Covid-19 lockdown measures/ Quarantine measure have impacted the children of India in terms of violation of their rights, 64.6% of the participant agreed with the statement, 29.2% answered with a neutral approach stating 'Maybe' while 6.3% of the participants denied any impact on the rights of children due to Covid.

Figure 1: **Major responsibility of protecting the rights of children lies with?**

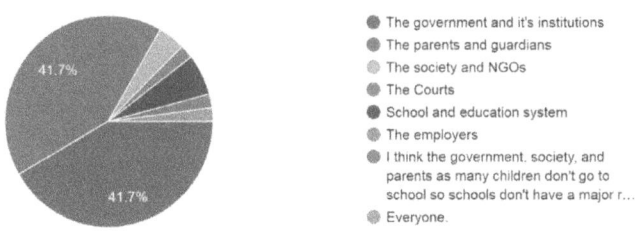

- According to the participants, on the question of who had the major responsibility of protecting the rights of the children. 41.7% agreed that the responsibility lied with the government and its institution while another 41.7% expressed that the responsibility was of the parents and guardian.

35

4.2% agreed that responsibility was of the Non-profit organizations and society while 6.3% agreed that the responsibility was on the schools and educational system. A minority of participant agreed that responsibility of protection of rights of children was on Courts (2.1%), Government, society and parents as a whole (2.1%) and everyone (2.1%).

*Figure 2:***Are you aware of any government policies introduced for the protection of children during covid-19?**

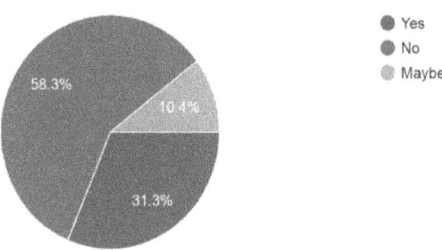

- A majority of the participant at 58.3% were not aware of any government policies which were introduced for the protection of children during the covid-19. 31.3% of the participant shared a positive response regarding the awareness while 10.4 % opted for a neutral option.

Figure 3: **Because of the Covid pandemic, which according to you has witnessed the most alarming increase?**

- The Participant at 38.3% identified that child abuse (including Physical and Sexual) witnessed the most alarming increase during the covid-19 Pandemic which was followed by absolute poverty (31.9%), Online Harassment (17%) while the minority in the participants were divided among Mortality rates (2.1%), absolute poverty and child abuse (2.1%), Anxiety disorder (2.1%), Domestic violence which may have impacted directly or indirectly (2.1) and child abuse together with online harassment (2.1%).

Figure 4: **Do you think Covid Lockdown measure have adversely affected children's education?**

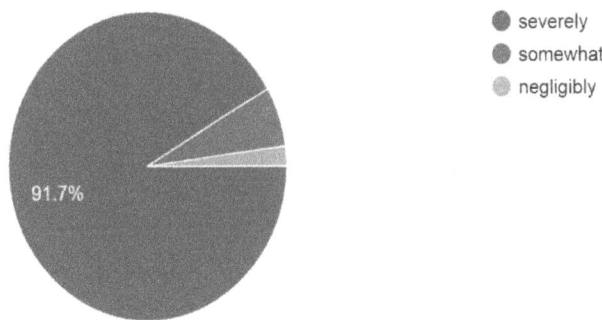

- A majority of 91.7% agreed that due to the Covid19 lockdown measure, children education had been severely impacted. 6.3% believed that the measure had somewhat impacted while a minority of 2.1% was of an opinion that education was negligently impacted.

Figure 5: **Rate the government efforts towards ensuring unhindered access to justice?**

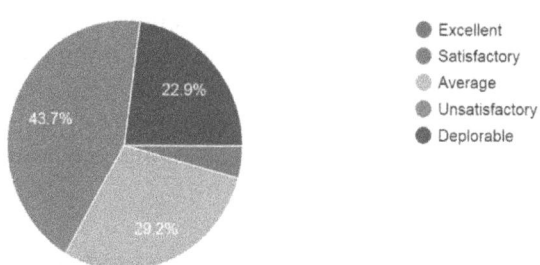

- Excellent
- Satisfactory
- Average
- Unsatisfactory
- Deplorable

- On the question of rating the government's effort to ensure unhindered access to justice, Majority (43.7%) agreed that the efforts were unsatisfactory, 29.2 % shared that the efforts were average while some participant shared that the efforts were deplorable (22.9%). A minority of 4.2% responded positively stating that government efforts were satisfactory.

Figure 6: **Biggest hindrance faced by the country in access to Justice?**

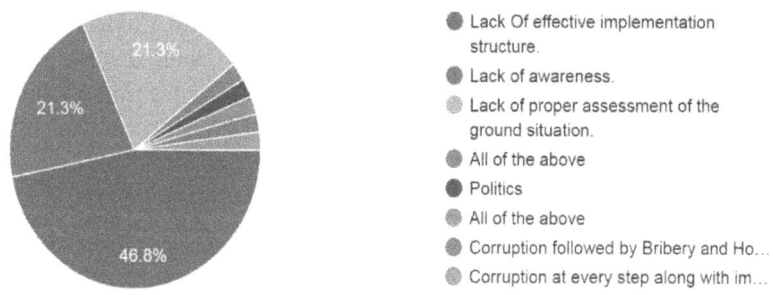

- Lack Of effective implementation structure.
- Lack of awareness.
- Lack of proper assessment of the ground situation.
- All of the above
- Politics
- All of the above
- Corruption followed by Bribery and Ho...
- Corruption at every step along with im...

- Lack of effective implementation structure was identified as the biggest hindrance faced by country in access of justice (46.8%). Followed by Lack of awareness (21.3%), Lack of proper assessment of ground level (21.3%). Minority of the participant varied in identifying different sources such as politics (2.1%), Corruption followed by bribery and hooliganism (2.1%), Corruption at every step of implementation (2.1%) and All of the mentioned causes (2.1%)

Figure 7: **What do you think of the Government's new policy to grant compensation and other benefits to children orphaned due to Covid?**

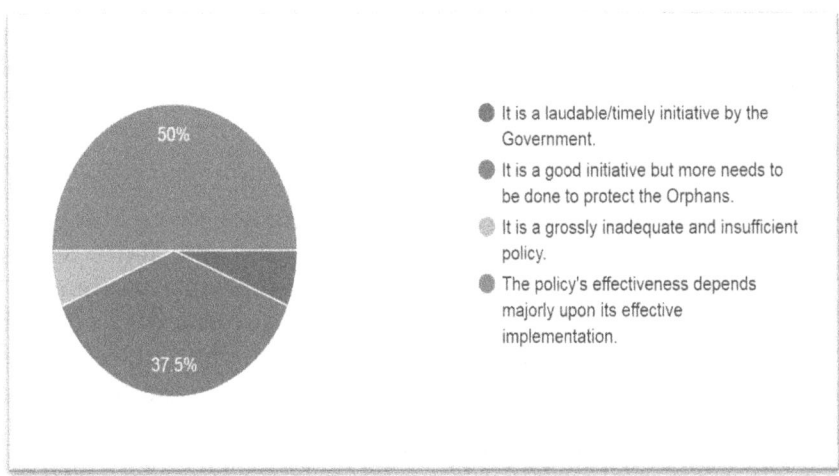

- It was observed that 50% of the total participants agreed that the recent order of the government to grant compensation and others benefits for children orphaned due to Covid-19 was a policy whose effectiveness depended majorly upon the effective implementation. While 37.5% believed that it was a good initiative but more needs to be to protect the Orphans. While a minor group agreed that the policy was a laudable/ timely initiative by the government (6.3%) and one group negated the policy as grossly inadequate and insufficient (6.3%).

Figure 8: **Government efforts to ensure hygiene and Covid protocol among children (especially disadvantaged group)**

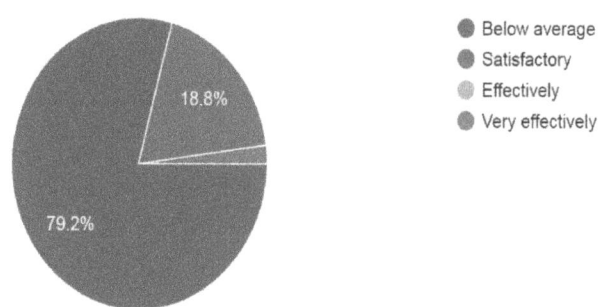

- On questions of awareness, 75% were not aware of any government measure to prevent violence and abuse among children during Covid, 20.8% were somewhat aware of the policies. Further on the question of government's effort to ensure proper hygiene and protocol among children (especially disadvantaged groups), 79.2% agreed that the efforts were below satisfactory, while only 18.8% agreed it was satisfactory with a minority of 2.1% claiming it to be very effective.

Figure 9: **Approach to be adopted in terms of child protection and access to justice policies?**

- 56.3% of the total participants agreed that there is a need to adopt a 'child welfare and sustainable development approach' in children protection and access to justice policies. 22.9% believed in the need for economic and social balance approach while 20.8% opted for an 'Utmost importance to child welfare approach'.

CONCLUSION: SUGGESTIONS

Children are the foundation blocks of the development of any society, thus it becomes imperative for the society as a whole to adopt policies to groom the children in a positive manner and to protect them from all kinds of offences/abuses. It is a very sensitive issue which demands an effective role of the government, integrated with social justice warriors. There are many steps which can be undertaken to ensure that the rights of the children are protected and they are granted unhindered access to justice, such as

o Accountability and effective implementation are the key elements for the success of any policy. There is an urgent need to create an independent and impartial unit which will act as a watch dog on the government and its efforts. Strengthening the current laws coupled with proper implementation is required.

o In order to have strong and effective implementation of child welfare legislations, there must be convergence of programs/schemes, regular monitoring and timely child rights impact evaluation studies with a clause of improvisation.

o There is a need to conduct large scale awareness programs not only about the concept of child rights but also regarding the policies and efforts which are taken by the government to ensure and protect the same. Such attempts can allow generating of a positive feedback and support of the community as a whole.

o It is the need of the hour to adopt a sustainable approach coupled with child welfare to encourage protection of all children and their generations to come. The sustainable development laws should be framed around ensuring violence prevention, decent work for children, abolishing poverty, providing good and quality education, ensuring no hunger and overall health of the children is up to the present international standards. The policy making should focus on accessing the ground situation and drafting such policies which will suit the socio- economic context of a particular region. Further, Accountability of each step of implementation is necessary.

o In order to prevent abuse and crime against children especially during the Covid-19, the Governments needs to think out of the box and adopt plans where the community members who are well versed with the realities are trained to impart child rights education at a micro level and serve as a bridge between the law enforcement agencies and the community.

o A periodical report assessing the changes, to monitor the activities and ensuring that the current policies are not stagnant is to be created. Such reports shall to made available to public in all local languages so that it reaches a wider audience.

o Special training should be imparted to the agencies (Police, Judiciary, Non-profits) directly involved in dealing with child issues in order to sensitize them regarding the fragility of the issue.

o Introduction of child rights as part of compulsory education curriculum.

o Encourage active role of children by IMUNs, debates, competitions so that children are given an active role in the decision making and are not reduced to mere objects.

o Covid-19 can be taken as an opportunity to identify the flaws in the current system and to rectify the same. The pandemic has allowed the surfacing of the population which was almost invisible (such migrant children, queer children etc.)

- Family based care agendas should be promoted as an alternative as the normal life has become confined to one's family.
- The pandemic has positively allowed people to recognize the importance of Mental health as well as identified domestic violence as a problematic phenomenon. This opportunity can be used to create awareness and adopt major policies to ensure that the awareness of the masses is channelized in a more concrete form.
- Special attention needs to be given to children who are at a comparative disadvantage including children suffering from absolute poverty, children dwelling in conflict zones, juvenile children, queer children and children of sex workers etc.
- The main focus of UNCRC is the importance of child participation in decision making, this area has often been neglected and special focus in this area is essentially required.
- There is a need to establish a strong and effective intra agency mechanism between the departments/agencies who are involved and working directly or indirectly with the welfare of child population.
- There is a need to increase the annual child Development Budget
- As per NEP 2020, Anganwadi centers need to impart both nutrition as well education, to ensure the same regular assessment and evaluation of ICDS program is required.
- There is a need to ensure best interests of children at every stage of their development and to strengthen the community-based child protection system.
- To strengthen the Child protection system and proper mapping of children in need of care and protection.
- Special All-round insurance schemes for children.
- It is true that Rome was not build in a day, but with consistent efforts and effective accountability the need of ensuring a safe and secure environment to children can be diligently satisfied.

REFERENCES

- https://www.google.co.in/amp/s/www.bbc.com/news/world-asia-india-54186709.amp. (Last visited 8:45 AM (IST), dated 2-August-2021)
- https://www.google.co.in/amp/s/www.savethechildren.in/news/india-covid-spike-further-risks-childrens-education-mental-

health-save-the-children/%3famp. (Last visited 2:57 PM (IST), dated 5- August-2021)

o https://www.google.co.in/amp/s/www.thehindu.com/news/national/coronavirus-lockdown-govt-helpline-receives-92000-calls-on-child-abuse-and-violence-in-11-days/article31287468.ece/amp/. (Last visited 5:23 PM, (IST), dated 6-August-2021)

o https://www.google.co.in/amp/s/www.tribuneindia.com/news/nation/take-care-of-children-orphaned-by-covid-supreme-court-directs-states-259855. (Last visited 9:30 AM (IST), dated 7-August-2021)

o https://www.ohchr.org/en/professionalinterest/pages/crc.aspx. (Last visited 3:47 PM (IST), dated 8-August ,2021)

o https://www.unicef.org/rosa/media/14096/file/Case%20Study%20-%20Bangladesh%20and%20India%20-%20The%20Importance%20of%20Child%20Helplines%20During%20the%20Time%20of%20COVID-19.pdf. (Last visited 6:15 PM(IST), dated 9- August-2021)

o https://www.unicef.org/rosa/press-releases/10-million-additional-girls-risk-child-marriage-due-covid-19. (Last visited 7:02 (IST), dated 9-August-2021)

EXPLORING THE ROLE OF LOCAL INITIATIVES OF INDIA IN ACHIEVING SUSTAINABLE DEVELOPMENT GOAL NO. 4

Rabiya Joshi[89]

Abstract

"Education is the most powerful weapon which you can use to change the world"
– Nelson Mandela

Sustainable development goal No. 4- ***Ensure inclusive and equitable quality education and promote lifelong learning opportunities for all*** is one of the most cardinal and paramount goal out of the 17 Sustainable Development Goals pursued avidly across the world. Education forms the very basis of development of any individual, community, and country. Every year millions of campaigns are held globally to stress upon the need of ensuring education for all. So, what makes education a necessity? Is it the employment opportunities or self-awareness or better decision making or capacity building or economic growth or human resource development? The reason be any of them, the results of inclusive and equitable education for all are far-reaching.

In this policy paper, I shall delve into some of the local initiatives by individual organizations of India in contributing towards SDG No. 4. Further I shall also highlight the significance of such concentrated efforts in a country like India, where there are religious, economical, caste and language barriers and how such initiatives have been successful in contributing towards Goal No. 4.

The research methodology shall be a combination of doctrinal method of analysing secondary data available in journals and online databases as well as empirical research by including the achievements of some of the local initiatives of India.

The policy outcomes I aim to reach can be summarized as:

---

[89] Student at University Institute of Legal Studies, Panjab University, Chandigarh, India.

45

- How a formal school/university education is required in tandem with localised efforts to achieve 'inclusivity'.
- How in a diversity-rich country like India, education is still a luxury for many, and 'equitable' education is possible only when privileged individuals work towards realizing this goal.
- How feasible is the implementation of the goal of 'promoting life-long learning opportunities for all' considering peculiar circumstances of India and lack of primary education in a significant portion of population.
- What role can the central and state governments play in promoting and assisting such initiatives.

India's greatest asset is its enormous population and in today's date almost all the economists of the world unanimously agree that human resource is the most invaluable resource for any country. So, this policy paper shall be an attempt to cover the role played by non-governmental bodies and make recommendations for the government and individuals to play an active role in effectuating this objective of converting 'potential manpower' into 'manifest human resource' of the country.

Key Words: SDG 4, Inclusivity, lifelong learning, NGOs, education.

Introduction

The Sustainable Development Goals or Global Goals forming part of Agenda 2030 for Sustainable Development consists of 17 interlinked goals designed to achieve universal, equitable and holistic development of all. All the goals have been envisaged keeping in mind need and necessity of their implementation. No specific goal is more urgent than others, rather all goals are crucial for individual as well as socio-economic growth.

- If poverty is reduced (SDG 1) but there is no responsible management of production and consumption (SDG 12), there could be a relapse of the problem.
- Similarly effective control of climate change (SDG 14) necessitates protection of life on land (SDG 15) and life below water (SDG 14).

- o Furthermore, for ensuring reduced inequalities (SDG 10) and fortifying peace and justice (SDG 16), gender equality (SDG 5) and **quality education** (SDG 4) are indispensable.

Quality education under SDG 4

"Education enables upward socioeconomic mobility and is a key to escaping poverty."[90]

This definition of Education specifies the function of education as an upward socioeconomic mobility and defines Education as a key to escaping poverty. Definitely, Education does both. However, I consider *education as a process of upskilling oneself.* Anything that uplifts one's mental aptitude to more progressive, scientific, and logical is education. Furthermore, education not only comprises of formal school/institutional education, but also:

- o The values/moral education a person receives at home and during social interactions. Such education, often considered too prosaic to be considered an education, does serve an essential function, that is imparting social and interpersonal skills.
- o The skills which though not 'labelled' as education, helps a person survive. For instance, the art of cutting bamboo trees (which can be used for making furniture) is certainly an education because it is a know-how which helps one earn and survive.
- o Formal/informal education conferred at NGOs targeting a specific weaker section of society like children, girls, specially abled, minority religions, linguistically bereft, etc.
- o The focus of this paper shall be the role played by NGOs in imparting education furthering SDG 4. Chiefly, SDG 4 aims to *"ensure inclusive and equitable quality education and promote lifelong learning opportunities for all."*

It includes 10 sub-targets:

1) Free primary and secondary education. (Target 4.1)

---

[90] Sustainable Development Goals, (2021, August 20) *Quality Education.* Retrieved from https://www.un.org/sustainabledevelopment/education/

This mandates provision of 12 years of free, completely funded by government, comprehensive, fair, quality primary and secondary education– of which minimum 9 years are compulsory, prompting significant learning results – ought to be guaranteed for all, without discrimination.[91]

2) **Equal access to quality pre-primary education. (Target 4.2)**

The provision of no less than 1 year of free and compulsory quality pre-primary education is encouraged, to be conveyed by well-trained teachers, alongside early childhood development and care.[92]

3) **Equal access to affordable technical, vocational, and higher education. (Target 4.3)**

It is essential to remove barriers related to accessibility to technical training, skills development and secondary and tertiary levels of education reaching to university level to achieve the goal of lifelong learning for adults. Thus, the provision of tertiary education should be made progressively free, in line with existing international agreements.[93]

4) **Increase the number of people with relevant skills for financial success. (Target 4.4)**

- o **Access:** This sub-goal aims to expand equitable access to TVET while ensuring the quality. Diversification and increase of learning opportunities by using wide range of education and training modalities so that all youth and adults, especially girls and women, can acquire relevant knowledge, skills and competencies for decent work and life.
- o **Skills acquisition:** Apart from work-specific skills, emphasis should also be placed on developing cognitive and non-cognitive/transferable skills, such as problem solving, critical thinking, creativity, teamwork, communication skills and

---

[91] The SDG-Education 2030 Steering Committee (2021, August 19) *Sustainable Development Goal 4 (SDG 4).* Retrieved from https://sdg4education2030.org/the-goal
[92] *Ibid.*
[93] *Ibid.*

conflict resolution. Such skills can be used across a range of occupational fields and in everyday life.[94]

5) Eliminate all discrimination in education. (Target 4.5)

- o **Inclusion and equity:** All people, irrespective of sex, age, race, colour, ethnicity, language, religion, political or other opinion, national or social origin, property, or birth, as well as persons with disabilities, migrants, indigenous peoples, and children and youth, especially those in vulnerable situations or other status, should have access to inclusive, equitable quality education and lifelong learning opportunities.
- o **Gender equality:** All girls and boys, women, and men, should have equal opportunity to enjoy education of high quality, achieve at equal levels and enjoy equal benefits from education. Adolescent girls and young women, who may be subject to gender-based violence, child marriage, early pregnancy, and a heavy load of household chores, as well as those living in poor and remote rural areas, require special attention. In contexts in which boys are disadvantaged, targeted action should be taken for them. Policies aimed at overcoming gender inequality are more effective when they are part of an overall package that also promotes health, justice, good governance, and freedom from child labour.[95]

6) Universal literacy and numeracy. (Target 4.6)

The standards, methodologies and actions for this goal are supported by the contemporary comprehension of literacy as a continuum of proficiency levels. Consequently, action for this goal requires that all young people and adults across the world should have achieved relevant and recognized proficiency levels in functional literacy and numeracy skills that are equivalent to levels achieved at successful completion of basic education.[96]

7) Education for sustainable development and global citizenship. (Target 4.7)

---

[94] *Ibid.*
[95] *Ibid.*
[96] *Ibid.*

It is an undisputed fact that quality education impacts fulfilment of human rights, peace, and responsible citizenship from local to global levels, gender equality, sustainable development, and health. So, a progressive Education involving cognitive and non-cognitive aspects of learning needs to be imparted. The knowledge, skills, values, and attitudes required by citizens to lead productive lives, make informed decisions, and assume active roles locally and globally in facing and resolving global challenges can be acquired through education for sustainable development (ESD) and global citizenship education (GCED), which includes peace and human rights education, as well as intercultural education and education for international understanding.[97]

8) Build and upgrade inclusive and safe schools. (Target 4-A)

This includes:
- o adequate schools and infrastructure therein.
- o safe and inclusive environment promoting learning for all, regardless of social/financial background or minority/disability.[98]

9) Expand higher education scholarships for developing countries. (Target 4-B)

Scholarship programmes are a great incentive for students coming from developing countries to developed countries. This is because, in developing countries, the average spending capacity of families is low and affording the education in developed countries can be financially exhausting for them. Therefore, scholarships helps to ease their financial burden. Also under this goal, developed countries are encouraged to increase other forms of support to education. In line with the SDG 4 - Education 2030 focus on equity, inclusion and quality, scholarships should be transparently targeted at young people from disadvantaged backgrounds.[99]

10) Increase the supply of qualified teachers in developing countries. (Target 4-C)

- o [97] *Ibid.*
- o [98] *Ibid.*
- o [99] *Ibid.*

Well-qualified teachers are an important determinant for attaining SDG 4 sub-targets. So, to overcome uneven distribution and shortage of well-trained teachers:

- o Adequate number of teachers should be appointed.
- o Made sure that they are empowered and dedicated.
- o They are well-educated and well-trained for imparting quality education to young minds.
- o Effective governance and support within academic.[100]

These sub-goals under SDG 4 act as guiding principles for individual countries to frame policies keeping in mind the specific goal that is to be fulfilled, for example eliminating discrimination in education, free and compulsory education, universal literacy, etc. Also, these targets elucidate different facets of SDG 4, realization of which eventually leads to accomplishing of SDG 4.

Localised efforts achieving 'inclusivity'

Inclusivity an important component of SDG 4, is a broad term that entails *"inclusion of those who were excluded from education for long but also the ones who inadvertently could not yield the benefits of education."* India is a diverse country having 100s of languages and 1000s of communities. There are many inaccessible areas plagued with so many problems and lack of education is just one of them. In such circumstances NGOs play an active role to undertake the task of education and training in such regions. Localized organizations have two-fold benefits:

a) They have a target population, and they can accordingly formulate their action plan, language of instruction and level of teaching.
b) They are more accessible than formal educational institutions, do not have cumbersome formalities and are able to connect better with parents/guardians.

Teach for India Foundation is one such organization which identifies and recruits bright candidates as fellows every year. Fellows commit to teaching low-income schools for 2 years. The purpose is

---

[100] *Ibid.*

to ensure holistic development of students and to make an impact on the school and community through their micro-initiatives. The learning process in such initiatives is vice-versa, while the students get upskilled through quality education, the fellows are equipped with leadership skills and most fellows can bring about a macro-change as an educationist.[101]

Pratham, a learning organization was set up in 1995 to educate the children in the slums of Mumbai. Today, it has grown in scope and reach with a focus on high quality, low cost, and replicable interventions which addresses the lapses in the education system. With a mission of 'Every child in school and learning well,' the organization has addressed several issues such as learning levels, dropout rates, child rights, and teacher training. Their programs focus on education, vocational training, technology, vulnerable children, and research and advocacy.[102]

Nirnayam NGO is a charitable organization committed to empowering girl child from underprivileged sections. The purpose is to academically support and holistically develop the students. The various initiatives undertaken by this NGO are imparting English language skills, extra-curricular activities for developing logical thinking and creativity among girls and simplifying the subjects like Mathematics and Sciences in their native language. Till now this NGO has been able to assist 500+ girls from South India to progress in academics and various other non-scholastic activities.[103]

Minds and Souls is a foundation working for promoting education among those with special needs. This organization is fully equipped with the Pre School and School Session, providing education and training to all kinds of children and adults with Behaviour Problems and Multiple Disabilities like Autism, Slow Learners, ADHD, Mental Retardation, Down Syndrome, Hearing, Speech and Visual Impair-

---

[101] Teach for India Foundation, (2021, August 25) *Our Model.* Retrieved from https://www.teachforindia.org/our-model

[102] Pratham, (2021, August 25) *About us.* Retrieved from https://www.pratham.org/

[103] Nirnayam, (2021, August 25) *About us.* Retrieved from http://www.nirnayam.org/

ment, etc. Till now they have been able to assist 100s of students with disability in Kolkata, India.[104]

Lifelong learning opportunities

Another important facet of SDG 4 is lifelong learning opportunities. But why was the need for including this aspect felt? Wouldn't inclusive and equitable education suffice? Indeed not. Majority of the world and significant population of the India has been bereft of education. Be it quality education or quantity education. By quantity education I mean the years of exposure to education. For instance, an average girl in a backward Indian village would hardly be 3rd/4th pass and in many instances completely illiterate. Such individuals when grow up, find it hard to upgrade themselves as per the changing circumstances. Not only there are regional disparities between literacy rates but also gender disparities. The literacy rates in some of the backward states of India are still below 60% for men (Uttar Pradesh, Bihar, Rajasthan, Jharkhand) and for women they are lesser than 40% also. Thus, in such situations, local organizations can motivate these people towards education in indirect ways utilising their capabilities in best possible manner.

Nirantar, is one such organization which works for promoting literacy, health education and vocational training among women from rural India since 1993. Women are also trained in specialised skills of writing so to enable them to undertake reporting, editing, and production of educational materials and to produce their own newspapers and booklets.[105]

Doon Vocational Education Society in Himachal Pradesh, India expertise in matters affecting the region, like art & culture, education & literacy, environment & forests, legal awareness & aid, Panchayati Raj, vocational training. Local people are made cognizant (by way of education) of the matters affecting their environment, cul-

---

[104] Minds and Souls, (2021, August 25) *Minds and Souls: An introduction.* Retrieved from https://www.mindsandsouls.org/index.html
[105] Nirantar Trust, (2021, August 25) *About us.* Retrieved from http://www.nirantar.net/

ture, and heritage, so that they become better participants in preservation of the same.[106]

Case study: In a story from Punjab, India, a girl was forced to drop out from school in 7th standard because of economic restraints. After almost 22 years, she had a daughter of same age as she was when she quit the school and seeing her study, she felt the zeal to continue her education and approached her daughter's school. The school authorities though initially reluctant, later agreed for letting her continue the education. After 10 years she and her daughter were together appointed as teachers in a primary school of the area.

So, its conspicuous that how lifelong learning opportunities have opened various avenues for middle aged groups and how despite abundant manpower, India has not been able to put it into use. *Its high time that instead of exploiting natural resources, countries start employing human resources.*

However, there are various factors that are conducive to ensure life-long learning, like:

a) Vocational courses training individuals in non-quintessential fields.
b) Equality in Employment opportunities, that is, no discrimination based on age. Many a times, lifelong learning in hampered because of non-employability.
c) Sciences training, including opportunities in technical fields and medical.
d) Safe and supportive environment in education centres.
e) It ought to be realized that education not just consists of formal school education, but also upskilling oneself through learning countless other skills like pottery, cookery, art, music, dance, etc. Many NGOs and smaller groups have been successful in imparting vocational training, rendering the young population employable. Their contribution towards SDG 4 is truly invaluable.

---

[106] NGO Foundation, (2021, August 25) *Doon Vocational Education Society Society Information.* Retrieved from https://www.ngofoundation.in/ngo-directory/doon-vocational-education-society-society-in-baddi-himachal-pradesh_i12985

Recommendations for governments

The commendable role of local initiatives in human development is evident. However, equally evident are the limitations and challenges faced by them. Therefore, in this section, I have suggested some measures which can be undertaken to counter these challenges.

i. One of the serious issues that numerous NGOs face is an absence of funds. This implies that for each kid that they educate, there are many kids that they cannot accommodate.

The long title of **The Right of Children to Free and Compulsory Education Act, 2009**[107] is *"An Act to provide for free and compulsory education to all children of the age of six to fourteen years."* Under Section 7 and 8 of the Act, the duties of government towards ensuring fulfilment of this Act's objectives are mentioned. These duties also include preparation and allocation of funds. As elaborately discussed in previous sections, the role played by local initiatives in exemplary, so according to me, these sections should be put into use to compensate for insufficient funds in certain bona fide NGOs.

Similarly in **The Rights of Persons with Disabilities Act, 2016**[108], under Section 86 and 87 National Fund for Persons with Disability has been established. This fund can be used to aid NGOs working in specialized field of disability education.

It is apparent that schools and colleges alone cannot ensure equitable education in a diverse country like India. Therefore, increasing the funding by government can yield positive results.

ii. Another factor which increases the significance of NGOs is the ability of NGOs to overcome failings in formal education (students being enrolled and not attending the schools). Such problems are effectively controlled by NGOs as they work on mutual trust between parents and NGO/Students and NGO. There is no compulsion

---

[107] The Right of Children to Free and Compulsory Education Act, 2009, (Act 35 of 2009) § 7 and § 8 http://www.bareactslive.com/ACA/ACT959.HTM
[108] The Rights of Persons with Disabilities Act, 2016, (Act 49 of 2016) § 86 and § 87 http://www.bareactslive.com/ACA/act2982.htm

or authoritarianism, and children feel more confident while attending such organizations for education. **Therefore, governments should promote such organizations actively by recognition on National Television and passively by funding.**

iii. Even though several organizations are solely dedicated to girl education, many people are still reluctant to get their girls educated. Unawareness and ignorance regarding importance of education is still widespread in many parts of India. **So, to combat this problem, combined effort from State, Central and local governments along with NGOs can help raise awareness amongst masses.**

iv. **Educational organizations be exempted from all kinds of taxes.** Though taxes are essential for the government treasury, the vision of these NGOs is equally paramount. So, the governments should avoid imposing any kind of tax liability on them. Further, essential services like electricity, water, infrastructure, food grains and other commodities can be provided to them at subsidized rates. This way, these organizations will be able to spend the maximum on implementation of SDG 4.

v. **In addition to funding, it is equally important for governments to stay vigilant.** This task of monitoring the activities of NGOs from time to time can be done by local governments with assistance from State governments. The purpose is to avoid wasteful spending of the government money; therefore, unethical practices and unscrupulous organizations must be detected by regular inspection.

vi. Last but not the least, the sphere of education should not be restricted, by age or in terms of opportunities. Every human is a human resource and effectuating their resourcefulness is imperative for development of any country. **Therefore, steps should be taken in collaboration with regional people and local organizations to make lifelong learning opportunities a living reality.**

References

https://www.ngofoundation.in/ngo-directory/doon-vocational-education-society-society-in-baddi-himachal-pradesh_i12985
https://sdg4education2030.org/the-goal
http://www.bareactslive.com/ACA/act2982.htm

http://www.bareactslive.com/ACA/ACT959.HTM
http://www.nirantar.net/
https://www.mindsandsouls.org/index.html
http://www.nirnayam.org/
https://www.pratham.org/
https://www.teachforindia.org/our-model

PRIMARY SCHOOLS - EQUITABLE DEVELOPMENT IN RURAL INDIA

Nikitha A

H. H. The Maharaja's Government Law College, Ernakulam,   M G University, India

EXECUTIVE SUMMARY

The education sector started facing trying times to cope up with the needs of the 'new normal' situation which is consequent to the pandemic outbreak which calls for the need of implementing SDG 4. The magnitude of the problem is high in rural areas as the substitute digital learning pedagogy adopted by the institutions was on halt due to obstacles like isolation, lack of accessibility to digital instruments, lack of knowledge on its usage, etc. This deprives the students of their Right to Education which is a fundamental right guaranteed by the Constitution of India. In this context, the state must address the situation and provide every student equitable access to digital facilities and redesign avenues of quality education.

The growing technology-driven spectrum requires the digital gap to be filled. The pandemic necessitated the use of digital learning methodologies. The no. of rural government schools adhering to computer-based technology is very low. Although proper infrastructure facilities are provided, only less focus is given on the availability of computer systems. Moreover, the primary focus of laws is on offline classrooms and hardcopy-based learning. Hence, a law promoting a digitalized environment to seek better development is to be enacted.

State action, however, acts as a catalog in initiating equitable growth. But, the prevalent laws, as a framework, are less effective in engaging an equitable development. The qualitative aspect (learning outcome) is expected to rise by enhancing the quantitative figures (enrollment rates, distribution of hardcopies, etc.). In the traditional and common pedagogy- teachers have a face to face interaction with students. The teacher is primarily assigned to manage a class of students. The law although mandates minimum teaching hours, nothing is prescribed in ensuring this. The lack of a system of checks and balances and transparency is visible. Hence, an inevitable measure must be the holistic development of schools in rural areas. In this paper, an analysis of the laws is made, and the extent of their implementation is also looked at.

Keywords: Primary education, Equity, rural schools, primary students, Digital learning.

INTRODUCTION

CONTEXT

The paper addresses equitable development of rural government schools and sets out the role of the legal framework and policy proposals of the government in the transformation of students and schools. The introductory chapter looks at the effect of the pandemic and possible reasons for the outcome. The second chapter delves into the legal framework and policies and cites where it is ineffective. The third chapter analyses the state of primary stakeholders of the sector. The last chapter states the recommendations.

INEQUALITY IN THE SECTOR

The right to education is considered a fundamental human right by international instruments. Providing education is a primary duty of the state.[109] Private unaided, government-aided, and government schools provide education to the majority. While most private schools are affiliated with CBSE, Government schools are mostly affiliated with State/ ICSE boards. The quality of education differs in both private and government schools. In India, over 90 percent of the rural schools at the primary level are being run by the government[110] An assumption can be that more than 70% of the families

---

[109] CESCR, General Comment n°13 para. 4

[110]Avantika Pandey. (2020, 27 July). GROWTH OF EDUCATION: RURAL INDIA.SCICOMM. https://scicomm.in/ education/growth-of-education-rural-india/

send their children to such schools, which still need some key facility upgrades.[111]

The accessibility to quality education signifies an inequality trend of location, economic category, social group (caste, religion), and gender.[112]This trend leads to wider gaps between rich and poor that compromise social mobility. Such inequality is not inevitable but rather depends on policy decisions.[113] The present law outlines a more exclusive education. It is requisite to address deeper issues like ensuring attendance and active participation of enrolled students, recognizing the students' physical, cognitive, and emotional element, the inclusion of the displaced, dropped out and Children with Disabilities, and an emergency to increase the infrastructure of primary schools in rural areas.

REVERBERATIONS OF THE PANDEMIC

The pandemic is said to have shown the reality of the vulnerability of the rural education system.[114] The challenges faced in this direction are one, 'learning outcome' from digital learning, two, the 'post-pandemic improvement' of rural schools, and three, ensuring the protection of child rights. With a paradigm shift in the pedagogy and the learning methods, the students are more prone to having in-

---

[111] Unni. Geetha (2021,29 August). Personal interview [Personal interview].

[112] Sushrut Desai(n.d.). Gender Disparity in Primary Education: The Experience in India https://www.un.org/en/chronicle/article/gender-disparity-primary-education-experience-india
[113] Jo Walker, Caroline Pearce, Kira Boe, Max Lawson. (17 September 2019) The power of education to fight inequality. Oxfam International.https://www.oxfam.org/en/research/power-education fight-inequality

[114] Kanchan Rai. (2020 December 20). It's not just adults who are stressed; children are, too!., The Indian Express. https://indianexpress.com/article/parenting/blog/its-not-just-adults-who-are-stressed-children-are-too-7112614/

creasing learning problems, both mental[115]and cognitive and the extreme, dropping out at a very young age (post-primary period).'[116]

The RTE Act and government programs like the Sarva Shiksha Abhiyaan (SSA) played a role in ensuring over 99.21 percent attendance in primary schools.[117] But, with the closure of schools, a significant number of students; were left unenrolled. There is a decrease in enrollment up to 5.3 percent compared to 1.8 percent in 2018.[118] The pandemic had a vibrant effect on various factors affecting the wellbeing of children, including the lack of learning materials (both online and offline materials), resulting in reduced learning outcomes. Remoteness triggered mental health issues, malnutrition, and inclination to work as child labour (or of any other sort).

A clear shift from private to government schools is there among both boys and girls between 2018 and 2020. The reason can be financial distress or permanent closure of schools.[119] This also affixes the public education domain to incorporate a more flexible yet impactful approach to raising learning outcomes. During the pandemic, extensive steps were opted by the respective state governments to provide learning materials like textbooks, worksheets, TV programs,

---

[115] Govindraj Ethiraj (2021 30 July) 'Schools Must Reopen For Children's Mental Wellbeing, To Narrow Digital Learning Gap' https://www.indiaspend.com/indiaspend-interviews/schools-must-reopen-for-childrens-mental-wellbeing-to-narrow-digital-learning-gap-764442

[116] Unni. Geetha (2021, August 29th). Personal interview [Personal interview].

[117] Ministry of Human Resource Development (2018) Sarva Shiksha Abhiyan (SSA): https://archive.pib.gov.in/ndagov/Comprehensive-Materials/compr10.pdf

[118] ASER Centre (2020 October 28, 2020) Annual Status of Education Report (Rural) 2020 Wave 1 http://img.asercentre.org/docs/ASER%202021/ASER%202020%20wave%201%20%20v2/aser2020wave1report_feb1.pdf

[119]Ibid

radio programs, and online sessions (transacted in regional languages).[120]

These suggest a better mechanism to introduce an extensive usage of technology in pedagogy along with traditional methods.

ANALYSING THE LEGISLATIVE HISTORY

With over 27% of the population being 14 years and below[121], India, a welfare state, has a positive obligation to provide free and compulsory education. A Fundamental Right guaranteed under Article 21A to provide Free and compulsory education to children aged 6-14 years, a directive principle of state policy envisaged under article 45 enacted the Right of Children to Free and Compulsory Education Act or The Right to Education Act in 2009. The Act aims at a prominent working of the Indian Education System by setting standards and describing duties allotted to institutions, holding a grievance mechanism. The National Education Commission or the Kothari commission set up by the Government of India had recommended numerous changes, including a classic restructuring to include a "neighboring school system.[122] It can equate to a means of spreading equitable education accessibility in rural areas.

The Sarva Shiksha Abhiyan, a campaign set up under the RTE Act to ensure 100 percent enrollment of students in the age gap between 6- 14 years. However, it has witnessed a gross enrollment ratio of over 100,[123] but around 35 million students in this age gap are not attending school.[124]The 'neighboring school system' is an approach

[120] *Ibid*

[121] UNESCO (n.d.) http://uis.unesco.org/en/country/in

[122] Ministry of Human Resource Department (1986) National Education Policy, 1986

[123] UNESCO Institute for Statistics (2020, September) 'School enrollment, primary (% gross)' - India.
https://data.worldbank.org/indicator/SE.PRM.ENRR?locations=IN

[124] Smile Foundation (n.d.) 'Our   Children'
https://www.smilefoundationindia.org/ourchildren.html

wherein a child is enrolled at a school merely one km away from the house. The local bodies have a statutory duty of only maintaining records of children under its jurisdiction (section 9(d) of the Right to Education Act, 2009). But the government has no standard transparent methods prescribed to ensure the implementation of norms. No data is mapping the enrollment rates according to the 'neighborhood schooling system'. The prerequisite for achieving high infrastructural standards in rural public schools will be to increase the investment in the sector. The country spent only 3.1% of its GDP on education in 2019-'20[125] against the 6% recommended by every national policy since 1968. The COVID 19 pandemic has necessitated increasing investment in the education sector, particularly in the e-learning domain. The budgetary allocation, while having approved FDI investing, slashed down by 6.1% compared to the year 2020-21.[126]

STATE OF THE BENEFICIARIES

Quality, Equity, and Equality[127] are to be the prime concerns in primary education. A deep divide between rural-urban and private-government schooling is visible. The difference in learning outcome manifests this. The below section discusses the state of the primary beneficiaries and how the framework falls short in addressing their needs.

STUDENTS

The performance of primary students more often in government schools has been below the expected level. Such a level of the out-

---

[125] The News Minute (2021, FEBRUARY 01) Union Budget 2021: Govt slashes allocation for education by 6.13%.
https://www.thenewsminute.com/article/union-budget-2021-govt-slashes-allocation-education-613-142548

[126] *Ibid*

[127] Naik, J. (1979). Equality, Quality, and Quantity: The Elusive Triangle in Indian Education. International Review of Education / Internationale Zeitschrift Für Erziehungswissenschaft / Revue Internationale De L'Education, 25(2/3), 167-185.http://www.jstor.org/stable/3443729

come can be due to various factors like - cognitive problem, teacher absenteeism, education and livelihood of parents, poor learning environment, not enrolled in the potential grade, less scope of revising, etc. The lack of interest and awareness of parents causing very little co-operation can be a reason for low outcomes. The Act only prescribes a few inputs; there is no mention of outputs. The quantitative result cannot yield qualitative growth (higher learning outcomes). The RTE Act seems to be more of a "right to access schooling" than a "right to education."[128]

A child is allotted a particular class according to age rather than the potential class of that child. The high curricular expectation sets high learning assumptions. For example, This assumption stretches to the belief that if children are in class 4, most of them would have successfully attained the learning expected of them in class 3.[129]
The percentage of children in rural government schools in Class 5 who can read at Class 2 level or better is only at 50.3%, with massive differences across states.[130]

This problem becomes significant in digital learning. The level of assimilation varies due to a lack of proper interaction. The learning environment differs from child to child. Further, to measure the learning outcome, tests aren't conducted periodically. Reading and pronunciation are also not assessed. This methodology cannot be

---

[128] Vishal Vasanthakumar (2021, Sep 10) The Right to Education Act has brought hope – but the pandemic has shown flaws that should be fixed

https://scroll.in/article/1004724/the-right-to-education-act-has-brought-hope-but-the-pandemic-has-shown-flaws-that-should-be-fixed

[129] ASER CENTRE (n.d.) POLICY BRIEF Key Findings from the Study Inside Primary Schools: Teaching and Learning in Rural India
http://img.asercentre.org/docs/Publications/Inside_Primary_School/Policy%20_brief/tl_study_policy_brief_oct25.pdf

[130] ASER Centre (2018) Annual Status of Education Report (Rural) 2018
http://img.asercentre.org/docs/ASER%202018/Release%20Material/aserreport2018.pdf

relied upon during the pandemic.[131] The feasibility of following the procedure mentioned in the RTE Act is uncertain. The unstable or no internet facilities in rural areas hinder the whole digital learning process. Around 50 percent of students are unable to access the net.[132]This amounts to a violation of their fundamental right to the Internet.[133]The government is unable to furnish instruments; this responsibility shifts to parents. Most likely, the parents purchase a smartphone. Those who were unable to buy were able to access from elsewhere. [134] The input proposed by the Act and what is put in by the government is not proportional to the output.

TEACHERS

The learning outcomes depend on the classroom engagement by teachers. The RTE Act mandates a classroom engagement for 200 working days per year and a minimum of 45 teaching hours per week. This standard is not converged. Burdening with governance/ administration works, inefficient schedules, no active filling of va-cancies are the grounds that remove accountability on teachers and deteriorate the quality of education. The absence of formal channels of communication (circulars) minimizes transparency in the system.[135] About 75 percent of such non-academic work was carried out during class hours, compared to 13.04% in private schools.[136]

---

[131] Unni. Geetha (2021, August 29th). Personal interview [Personal interview].

[132] Prashasti Awasthi (2021, February 17) Over 50% of students don't have access to internet: Survey
https://www.thehindubusinessline.com/news/education/over-50-of-students-dont-have-access-to-internet-survey/article33859585.ece

[133] Faheema Shirin v. State of Kerala (2019) W.P(C). No.19716/2019-L
https://indiankanoon.org/doc/188439981/

[134] ASER Centre (2021, January 31) ASER 2020 Wave1 report
http://img.asercentre.org/docs/ASER%202021/ASER%202020%20wave%201%20-%20v2/nationalfindings.pdf

[135] N Shobha. (2021, August 21). Personal Interview [Personal interview]

[136] Indira Patil (2020, 22 October.) Teacher accountability: Non-teaching

Inefficient scheduling further reduces the teaching hours: when other student activities get prioritized over learning.[137] The Act provides for the deployment of teachers for election purposes under section 27. During the pandemic, at the time of a panchayat election, the teachers were put into a high-risk task when appointed as booth-level officers.[138]

Students in low socioeconomic areas experience more teacher absences. Around 2.5- 5 percent of teachers were on truancy.[139]The Act under section 24(2) specifies a disciplinary action against the teacher committing default. However, letters by principals reporting such default are not taken into consideration often.[140]

SCHOOLS

The learning environment dominates the learning culture in a school. The students enrolled in rural government schools face suboptimal schooling experience and poor learning outcomes. [141] Vari-

---

work over classroom engagement. Ideas For India.https://www.ideasforindia.in/topics/human-development/teacher-accountability-non-teaching-work over-classroom-engagement.html

[137] *Ibid*

[138] Scoop Whoop Unscripted (2021, May9). Investigating Deaths of 700 Teachers in UP Panchayat Polls Ground Report [Video]. YouTube. https://www.youtube.com/watch?v=MruSP_OpRWU

[139] Azim Premji University (2017, 21 Apr) Teacher absenteeism study https://archive.azimpremjiuniversity.edu.in/SitePages/pdf/Field-Studies-in-Education-Teacher-Absenteeism-Study.pdf

[140] BBC (2014, 7 August) India school teacher 'absent for 23 years' https://www.bbc.com/news/world-asia-india-28684751

[141] Tanoj Meshram (2021, 7 January) Reimagining rural public schools for equal and quality education for all https://timesofindia.indiatimes.com/blogs/sharp-tongue/reimagining-rural-public-schools-for-equal-and-quality-education-for-all/

ous infrastructural facilities are a contributing factor. But the inputs provided through the government funds are not equivalent to the output measured. 2.9% of schools function without drinking water facilities, 18.52% without electricity, 4.18% with no boys' toilets, and 2.64% without girls' toilets, 10.9% had no medical checkups for students.[142] These are some of the basic facilities which are in schedule of the Act. It is an obligation on the state and local bodies to ensure such facilities are available. But school closures are more common than school repairs amounting to non-compliance with sections 8(d) and 9(f) of the RTE Act, 2009.

Hence, India needs fundamental restructuring of its public school system and not its abandonment in favor of the choice of private schools.[143]The exclusion one is facing cannot be compensated by the privilege one is having.

Although in recent times of remote schooling, a change in roles was visible where the state government ensured availability of learning resources, with the school faculties remotely functioning. But the schools were not equipped for this as only 30.03% of the schools had computers and 11.58% had internet access.[144]

School development is in section 5.9 of the National Education Policy, 2020, but what is required is a stricter mechanism on the assessment of schools and the implementation of rules.

---

[142] Department of School Education and Literacy, Ministry of Human Resource Development. (2020) June. India Report Digital Education. https://www.education.gov.in/sites/upload_files/mhrd/files/India_Report_Digital_Education_0.pdf

[143] Tanoj Meshram (2021, 7 January) Reimagining rural public schools for equal and quality education for all https://timesofindia.indiatimes.com/blogs/sharp-tongue/reimagining-rural-public-schools-for-equal-and-quality-education-for-all/

[144] Department of School Education and Literacy, Ministry of Human Resource Development. (2020) June. India Report Digital Education. https://www.education.gov.in/sites/upload_files/mhrd/files/India_Report_Digital_Education_0.pdf

CONCLUSION

Education is one of the tools to increase the standard of living, develop an equitable and just society, all necessary for the development of a country. With over 65.074 percent of the population in rural areas [145] and considering the precarious situation, it is necessary to focus on rural areas. The children are made to help their parents at a very young age. This increases the chances of them skipping classes. While the mid-day meal scheme acted as a magnet in pulling children into schools, the current pandemic situation made them more vulnerable. An inequality, inequity, and low quality were visible, this sheds light on the existing loopholes of the system and education poverty. Such a condition was visible among the beneficiaries of the sector. The students are unable to get quality education, the teachers are unable to engage classrooms and the schools are lacking standard facilities. The students have to engage in a poor classroom environment. They also have to face teacher absences. The teachers are overburdened with administrative work which is usually completed during class hours. Rural public schooling falls far behind its urban public and private counterparts. Inefficient working is the fundamental reason.

The country falls short of a strict regulation controlling the working of the system. Poor communication lines contribute to this. The Act itself does not create a balance between many elements. It can be amended to include a more procedure-based system. A transparent, cooperative, and consultancy-based system is essential for implementing policies that can initiate change.

---

[145] World Bank. (2018). Rural population (% of total population) - India. The World Bank.https:// data.worldbank.org/indicator/SP.RUR.TOTL.ZS?locations=IN

RECOMMENDATIONS

Sl. no.	Provisions in the Act	Suggestions
	Sections 8(d) and 9(f) of the Act imposes a responsibility on appropriate government and local bodies to provide the required material to the students of their jurisdiction.	Reducing digital disparity by providing internet and improving the internet facilities to a more speedy and reliable network connection. Digital Literacy campaigns are to be conducted at panchayats where people have received a device under the government scheme.
	----	'Fund a Child' policy can be adapted for students in rural primary schools. The child's education can be funded by an individual/organization through a portal. This can result in an immense reduction in costs on the government and excess funds can be used for improving infrastructure. Moreover, this can be a more transparent system wherein individuals can keep an account and the funds can be properly utilized.
	Section 24(b) read with sections 24(c)and 29(2) mandates the teacher to complete a prescribed syllabus within a period.	Providing greater teaching autonomy and fairly lesser accountability for the efficient discharge of functions. This can enhance the learning of students as it provides a flexible approach.
	Section 9(b) of the RTE Act	Panchayat level surveys can be conducted annually on i) mapping the students to ensure the neighborhood schooling system is fol-

		lowed. ii) Out of school children and ensuring they are taught well. iii) Recognizing children who require funds.
	Section 10 of the Act mandates the parents to enroll their children in school.	To promote a learning environment at the house, awareness programs can be conducted among parents to make them realize their role in the child's education.
	Section 29(g) of the Act mandates the creation of such a learning environment making the child free of fear, trauma, and anxiety.	A counselor can be appointed in every 5 schools, who is responsible for monthly assessing the mental, cognitive, and emotional state of mind of children, who can submit a report and communicate to the teachers if any child needs attention.
	Section 27 of the RTE Act	Incorporating an 'administration department' with a minimum of 2 members in every school.
	Schedule to the RTE Act	In every panchayat, every school can submit its self-assessment i.e., self-evaluation by schools on drinking water facility, toilets, computer, internet, electricity, facilities, etc., maintenance of ideal PTR, and student report card and teacher performance based on classroom engagement and an official can verify it. This can be calculated on state- level and a School Grading System can be set up.
	Sections 8(d) and 9(f) of the Act imposes a responsibil-	The teacher can keep track of the attendance of students. Wherein, if a child is absent for more than a week,

	ity on appropriate government and local bodies to monitor the attendance of the students.	the parents can be communicated. And if for more than 2 weeks, immediate help can be assisted from the police department.

HUMAN TRAFFICKING– GLOBAL COMPARISON WITH SPECIAL FOCUS ON INDIA, UNITED STATES AND BANGLADESH

Ankita Sen
Amity University, Kolkata

ABSTRACT

People of conscience all across the world find today's extensive trafficking of men, women, and children intolerable. Standard techniques to preventing human trafficking, protecting and assisting trafficked people, and prosecuting criminals have made a simple but significant impact on the worldwide occurrence, but not nearly sufficient. That even one young person be denied the benefits of childhood, that one young woman be subjected to the brutal humiliation of sexual exploitation and that one man become the slave of a cruel taskmaster in another country are clear signals that we must renew both our resolve as well as our initiatives to protect those who are vulnerable. The United Nations Global Initiative to Fight Human Trafficking (UN. GIFT) was established out of a reinvigorated resolve by global leaders to stop human trafficking, one of the world's most severe breaches of human rights today. The United Nations Office on Drugs and Crime (UNODC) officially inaugurated it in March 2007, thanks to a substantial funding from the United Arab Emirates. GIFT is a call to action that reminds governments, civil society organisations, the media, the business community, and concerned citizens of their shared obligation to combat human trafficking, and that this struggle cannot be won or waged alone.

Keywords: human trafficking, sexual exploitation, extensive trafficking, severe breaches.

INTRODUCTION

Trafficking has been classified as the world's fastest expanding criminal industry and human trafficking being the world's third largest organised crime behind drugs and the arms trade. This paper addresses the International and Indian legal standards for trafficking of humans which has been further discussed with suggested solutions under several components which includes sex trafficking, labor trafficking, and organ trafficking but the law that prohibits it is the Immoral Trafficking Prevention Act (ITPA), which only prohibits it if it is done for the purpose of sexual exploitation. Further Section 370 and Section 370 (A) of Indian Penal Code 1860 has also been discussed along with considering the GLO Act (The Global Action to Prevent and Address Trafficking in Persons and the Smuggling of Migrants) - Islamic Republic of Pakistan which ensured a gender-sensitive and human-right based approach to Trafficking Persons (TIP) and Smuggling Persons (SOM) and providing better approach towards GLO Act- Bangladesh (2018-2022). According to the Walk Free Foundation Global Slavery Index 2017, India and the United States are home to millions of victims of human trafficking and are sometimes referred to as destination countries, or countries to which persons are trafficked. Bangladesh, on the other hand, is known to as a source country because the victims are frequently trafficked from these source countries. Hence, the researcher focused specifically on India, US and Bangladesh. Victims of human trafficking are abused and exploited in a variety of ways, which can lead to minor and serious psychological and physical attacks, as well as several diseases, particularly sexually transmitted diseases which can even result in death or permanent disability. The purpose of this study is to look into the reasons and mechanisms of human trafficking in India and United States, to investigate human trafficking-related offences, to propose human trafficking prevention measures in India, as well as to focus on international human trafficking treaties. The research is based on secondary data from the District Census Handbook, the Statistical Abstract State wise, the National Crime Record Bureau (NCRB), and the UNODC (United Nations Office on Drugs and Crime) Global Report on Person Trafficking, as well as data from books, articles, newspaper articles, and other web sources. The researcher has gathered the most relevant material using both qualitative and quantitative research methods, further analytical and conceptual methodologies have also been used. It has offered the distinctions between the reasons for varying human trafficking indexes in India and other countries, as well as the best feasible reformation proposals. Trafficking of humans still continues due to inadequate law enforcement; traffickers can earn large rewards under minimal risk and punishment. The researcher tries to enhance the Human Trafficking laws with this paper, so that they meet all the standards for combating human trafficking globally.

WHAT DOES HUMAN TRAFFICKING MEAN?

Human trafficking is the illegal use of force, deception, or compulsion to gain labour or a commercial sex act. Millions of men, women, and children are trafficked every year all across the world, particularly especially here in the United States. Victims might be of any age, ethnicity, gender, or nationality, and it can happen in Traffickers might use violence, manipulation, or false promises of well-paying jobs or romantic relationships to lure victims into trafficking situations.

Human trafficking is a covert crime since victims are often prevented from seeking aid due to language issues, fear of their traffickers, and/or fear of law enforcement.

To seduce their victims into work or commercial sexual exploitation, traffickers utilise force, deceit, or compulsion. They are looking for people who are vulnerable for a variety of reasons, such as psychological or emotional weakness, economic difficulty, a lack of social safety net, natural calamities, or political instability[146]. The mental anguish created by human traffickers can be so severe that many victims do not recognise themselves as victims or seek help, even in public places.

There are a lot of myths and misconceptions out there. The first step in identifying victims of human trafficking is to recognise key indicators, which can save a life. Almost every of the symptoms listed are present in every case of human trafficking, and the existence or disappearance of any of them is not proof of human trafficking.

The public's as well as the victim's protection is vital. Would not confront a suspected human trafficker or inform a victim of your concerns. It is the responsibility of enforcement agencies to investigate suspected human trafficking instances.

REASONS FOR HUMAN TRAFFICKING IN INDIA

Human trafficking, defined as the unlawful exchange_of individuals for the purposes of_commercial sexual exploitation servitude or

---

[146] https://www.dhs.gov/blue-campaign/what-human-trafficking

forced labour, is affects approximately 24.9 million people world-wide, with 8 million victims living across India's borders, according to the Global Slavery Index. There were 8,132 human trafficking incidents reported in India in 2016, up 20% from 2015, and 23,117 persons were rescued from the human trafficking system. 60 percent of those rescued were children, 55 percent were women and girls, 33 percent were trafficked for sexual services, and 45 percent were trafficked for forced labour. While extreme poverty, political instability, and war account for most of the overall prevalence of human trafficking, the reasons of human trafficking in India are more complex.

Gender-based discrimination, which is responsible for the deaths of approximately 239,000 girls under the age of five in India each year, is one of the causes of human trafficking in India. Male children are recognised extra important to the community than daughters, so gender discrimination is a cultural norm in India. Girls have severely restricted right to schooling in this patriarchal culture, tends to result in gender disparities in literacy rates and financial earning capacity.

As per the census of 2011, men had an 82 percent literacy level and women had a 65 percent literacy level, while men were paid 25% further than women in the 2013 census. The sex ratio in India is greatly distorted as a result of gender-based discriminatory treatment.

Since there are significantly more guys than young ladies in India. bride trafficking or the unlawful sale of women for the sacrament of procreation becomes more and more common in India. Bridal trafficking has been common in the more rural Northern states, where the sex ratio is higher than the national average[147]. And over 90% of women married in these Northern states have been sold from many other states at least three times, while also becoming brides as young as adolescence. Gender inequality in India has reinforced a societal framework that disproportionately benefits males against females to the moment of self, since men have been unable to find spouses, contributing to a need for human trafficking of Indian women for the point of marriage.

---

[147] https://theexodusroad.com/causes-effects-of-human-trafficking/

1) Sex Smuggling

Another reason for human trafficking in India is a lack of opportunity to support for one's family in India's underprivileged neighbourhoods, particularly for uneducated women. In India, just 43% of women employed in regular paid or salaried positions in 2012. In India, the majority of victims of sex trafficking are young, illiterate females from destitute families in rural areas. Despite the fact that poverty is reducing in India, 28 percent of the population still live-in abject poverty.

Human traffickers target poor communities because they frequently offer greater work possibilities or debt relief to entice victims. With little options to earn money, young women find it difficult to turn down offers like this. Because younger girls are assumed to be less likely to carry sexually transmitted illnesses, the average age of sex trafficking victims has decreased from 14 to 16 years.

2) Forced Labour/ Work trafficking

They lure victims from India's destitute rural communities, claiming squish payments at the end of their contracts. Workers are underpaid for their work, and terrible working conditions cause sicknesses, which lead to wage advancements and loan which maintain the labour in indebtedness to their contractors for the rest of their lives. Human trafficking for the purpose of forced labour. The majority of victims of this pervasive form of trafficking are from developing countries. They are lured and trafficked by fraud and duress, and they eventually work in slave-like surroundings in a range of jobs. Victims may be forced to work in agriculture, mining, fishing, or construction, as well as domestic servitude and other labour-intensive employment.

3) Human trafficking for the purpose of coerced criminal activity

The government strengthened anti-trafficking criminalization slightly, but they were still insufficient in comparison to the scope of the problem. Sex trafficking and other kinds of labour trafficking are now illegal in India. Theft, drug production, counterfeit products sales, and forced begging are just a few examples.

Trafficking charges including exploitation were criminalised under Section 370 of the Indian Penal Code (IPC), which encompassed any act of physical exploitation or any type of sexual exploitation, enslavement or practises similar to slavery, and servitude. The law makes no mention of labour trafficking[148]. For offences involving an adult victim, Section 370 imposed penalties ranging from seven to ten years in prison and a fine, and for offences involving a child victim, penalties ranging from ten years to life in prison and a fine; these penalties were extreme and, in the case of sex illegal trade, comparable to those imposed for other serious offences such as kidnapping. Section 370 needed a proof of assault, fraud, or compulsion to establish a child prostitution violation[149], which was inconsistent with international law and did not prohibit all forms of child sex trafficking. Sections 372[150] and 373[151] of the IPC, on the other hand, made it illegal to exploit children through prostitution without requiring proof of such methods, bridging this gap. These sections-imposed penalties of up to ten years in jail and a fine that were sufficiently severe and comparable to those imposed for other major crimes like kidnapping. The Scheduled Castes and Scheduled Tribes (Prevention of Atrocities) Act and the Bonded Labour System (Abolition) Act[152] (BLSA) both made bonded labour illegal, with penalties of up to five years in prison and three years in prison, respectively. The sanctions imposed by the BLSA were insufficiently severe. Police persisted to file trafficking cases under the Juvenile Justice Act and other sections of the IPC, which criminalised many forms of forced labour; however, these provisions were inconsistently enforced, and some of the penalties prescribed were insufficiently severe, allowing only fines or short prison sentences. Other legislation,

---

[148] https://www.legalserviceindia.com/legal/article-2334-kinds-of-human-trafficking.html

[149] https://www.interpol.int/en/Crimes/Human-trafficking/Types-of-human-trafficking

[150] https://indiankanoon.org/doc/1938563/#:~:text=%E2%80%94Whoever%20sells%2C%20lets%20to%20hire,to%20be%20likely%20that%20such

[151] https://indiankanoon.org/doc/530949/

[152]

https://labour.gov.in/sites/default/files/TheBondedLabourSystem(Abolition)Act1976.pdf

such as the Protection of Children from Sexual Offenses Act[153] (POCSO) and the Immoral Traffic Prevention Act (ITPA), made sex trafficking crimes illegal.

4) Women's trafficking for sexual exploitation

Every part of the world is affected by this common form of trafficking, whether as a sourcing, transportation, or destination country. Promises of good employment entice women and children from poor nations and marginalized sectors of society in wealthy nations to leave their families and migrate to just what they assume might be a great future.

Victims are frequently given fraudulent identification papers, and they are transported to the destination country via an organised network, where they will be coerced into sex trafficking and detained in inhumane conditions and unremitting fear.

5) Organ trafficking is a crime that occurs when people are trafficked for the purpose of removing organs

In several nations, transplant processing times are extremely long, and criminals have taken advantage of patients' and eligible donors' despair. Procedures may be performed out in secret and without any surgical follow-up, putting victims' health, if not their lives, in jeopardy.

The need for organ transplants is anticipated to rise as the population ages and the presence of diabetes rises in several affluent countries, making such offense much more expensive.

COMPARISON OF HUMAN TRAFFICKING BETWEEN INDIA, BANGLADESH AND UNITED STATES

Human trafficking in India

This definition in Section 370 not only perpetuates the conflation of human trafficking and sex work, but it also introduces new complications: the broad definition encompasses many people displaced by forced migration, denies aimed people's organisation, and provides the state and bureaucracy system and its organisations, in-

---

[153] https://wcd.nic.in/sites/default/files/POCSO%20Act%2C%202012.pdf

cluding the police, unregulated power. It also advocates for a criminalization strategy to combating human trafficking. The National Crime Record Bureau (NCRB)[154] of the Government of India gathers information about the current number of cases of human trafficking using this definition of 370. 95 percent of trafficked people in India are pushed into prostitution, according to statistics[155]. According to the NCRB, there are a total of 6,616[156] human trafficking instances documented in India, with sex trafficking being the most common. The credibility of these figures is questioned because they are based on the concept of trafficking in Section 370[157], which amalgamates sex work with trafficking. Since both the ITPA and Section 370 allow it, these figures potentially include examples of adult sex workers who consented but were denied consent during anti-trafficking operations[158]. However, these data and laws place sex workers in a scenario where they are targeted selectively by anti-trafficking actors and actions.

Protection - India's needed to defend human trafficking victims differ by state, but many remain ineffective. Bonded labour victims are entitled to a monetary compensation from the central government for rehabilitation, even though the policy is implemented unevenly around the country because government officials do not actively seek out and rescue bonded workers, fewer victims obtain support. Although some authorities give services to bonded labour victims, the majority of protective services are provided by non-governmental organisations. Indian victims trafficked abroad for forced labour or commercial sexual exploitation are not protected by the central government. Indian diplomatic posts in destination countries may provide temporary sanctuary to victims of human

---

[154] https://ncrb.gov.in/en/node/2986

[155] https://blogs.lse.ac.uk/humanrights/2021/02/11/human-trafficking-in-india-how-the-colonial-legacy-of-the-anti-human-trafficking-regime-undermines-migrant-and-worker-agency/

[156]https://ncrb.gov.in/sites/default/files/crime in india table additional table chapter reports/Table%2014.1 5.pdf

[157]https://indiankanoon.org/doc/1153041/#:~:text=%E2%80%94Whoever%20imports%2C%20exports%2C%20removes,also%20be%20liable%20to%20fine.

[158] https://en.wikipedia.org/wiki/Human trafficking in India

trafficking; but, once repatriated, neither the central government nor most state governments provide medical, psychological, legal, or reintegration aid. Section 8 of the ITPA (Immoral Traffic Prevention Act, 1956)[159] permits the arrest of women in prostitution. Although statistics on arrests under Section 8 are not kept, the government and some NGOs report that, through sensitisation and training, police officers no longer use this provision of the law; it is unclear whether arrests of women in prostitution under Section 8 have actually decreased. Because most law enforcement authorities lack formal procedures to identify trafficking victims among women arrested for prostitution; some victims may be arrested and punished for acts committed as a result of being trafficked.

Some foreign victims trafficked to India are not subject to removal. Those who are subject to removal are not offered legal alternatives to removal to countries in which they may face hardship or retribution. NGOs report that some Bengali victims of commercial sexual exploitation are pushed back across the border without protection services. The government also does not repatriate Nepali victims; NGOs primarily perform this function. Many victims decline to testify against their traffickers due to the length of proceedings and fear of retribution by traffickers those who are subject to removal are not offered legal alternatives to removal to countries in which they may face hardship or retribution.

Human trafficking in Bangladesh

In Bangladesh, Human trafficking is one of the most lucrative types of ill-conceived venture. The high benefit, just as the low punishment nature of illegal exploitation business, has made it more appealing to dealers (groups of thugs) and just as exceptionally enormous scope coordinated wrongdoing in Bangladesh (Chowdhury 2003).

It has been discovered that inside, most recent thirty years more than 1 million youngsters and ladies were carried out of the country[160]. The current UNICEF report uncovers that around 400 youngsters and ladies are dealt with every month. Another report uncov-

---

[159] https://indiankanoon.org/doc/27208336/

[160] https://fairbd.net/human-trafficking-in-bangladesh-an-overview/

ers that around 3 lac Women and kids who have a place with the age between 12 to 30 years of old were pirated to India alone from Bangladesh somewhat recently. The Pakistan-based Lawyers for Human Rights and Legal Aid in one of its reports distributed that around 200,000 ladies and young ladies who are the nationals of Bangladesh were exchanged Pakistan. Some other review says that the quantity of ladies and young ladies of Bangladesh in Pakistan is undocumented and it will go more than 250,000.

Bangladesh is a critical dealing centre that joins South Asia to Gulf district. The chief course what the dealers follow begins from Dhaka to Mumbai of India, Karachi of Pakistan and afterward Dubai. Human dealers utilize 20 travel guides situated in 16 locales toward sneak individuals from Bangladesh to India. Some other recently travel focuses have been found as of late to sneak individuals from Bangladesh to South – East Asian nations utilizing water courses. As per the UNHCR report inside most recent year and a half, till to date an absolute number of individuals 1.5 lac has been dealt by boats and ships through The Bay of Bengal. Inside the initial 3 months of 2015, roughly 25000 individuals, from different pieces of the nation, have been dealt utilizing Teknaf, Ukhia, Cox's Bazar Sadar and Maheshkhali focuses. As of late, on June 2015, Bangladesh Coast Guard group has saved 116 individuals from Bay of Bengal among whom 2/3 are 16 to 25 years of old.

In 2012, illegal exploitation took an awful scene with expanding number of focuses for dealing individuals utilizing water courses of the country from the Cox's Bazar, Teknaf, Maheshkhali and Ukhia region (ntv Bangladesh 2015). Considering that, every one of these data have been uncovered after the revelation of mass graves in Thailand.

Human trafficking in United States

Human exploitation casualties can be of all ages, race, nationality, sex, sexual direction, ethnicity, movement status, social foundation, religion, financial class, and schooling accomplishment level. In the United States, people powerless against illegal exploitation remember youngsters for the kid government assistance and adolescent equity frameworks, including child care; runaway and destitute youth; unaccompanied far off public kids without legitimate movement status; people looking for haven; American Indians and Alaska Natives, especially ladies and young ladies; people with substance use issues; racial or ethnic minorities; transient workers, remembering undocumented specialists and members[161] for visa programs for transitory labourers; unfamiliar public home-grown specialists in political families; people with restricted English capability; people with handicaps; LGBT+ people; and casualties of close accomplice viciousness or different types of abusive behaviour at home.

RECOMMENDATIONS AND SUGGESTIONS

Notwithstanding, picking gravity over activity isn't to the greatest advantage of casualties and overcomers of business sexual abuse and sex dealing of minors who are exposed to ongoing sexual double-dealing or of weak kids and young people whose double-dealing could be forestalled. In this manner, the advisory group features techniques for utilizing existing assets sooner rather than later, and desires solid and prompt activity to forestall, distinguish, and address these wrongdoings.

Suggestion 1: The Department of Justice, the Department of Health and Human Services, and the Department of Education, working with different accomplices, should expand attention to business sexual double-dealing and sex dealing of minors by supporting the turn of events, execution, and assessment of

• public, local, state, and nearby proof educated preparing for experts and others who regularly cooperate with kids and youths;
• explicit techniques for bringing issues to light among kids and teenagers.

Suggestion 2: All public, state, nearby, ancestral, and regional wards ought to foster laws and strategies that divert youthful casualties and overcomers of business sexual abuse and sex dealing from capture and indictment as lawbreakers or mediation as reprobates to frameworks, organizations, and administrations that are prepared to address their issues. Such laws ought to apply to all youngsters and youths under age 18.

---

[161] https://www.state.gov/humantrafficking-about-human-trafficking/

Suggestion 3: All public, state, neighbourhood, ancestral, and regional locales should survey, fortify, and carry out laws that hold exploiters, dealers, and specialists responsible for their part in business sexual abuse and sex dealing of minors. These laws ought to remember a specific accentuation for stopping interest.

Suggestion 4: The Department of Justice, the Department of Health and Human Services, and the Department of Education ought to team up and collaborate with others to execute a public exploration plan zeroed in on

• propelling information and comprehension of business sexual abuse and sex dealing of minors in the United States;
• creating powerful, youngster and juvenile focused, multisector intercessions intended to keep kids and teenagers from becoming casualties or exploiters and to help the individuals who have been taken advantage of; and
• creating systems and philosophies for assessing the viability of anticipation and mediation laws, strategies, and projects.

CONCLUSION

Basic liberties encapsulated in the Indian Constitution are legitimate. This load of rights presently has the help of countless global shows and common freedoms pledges managing basic liberties. Indeed, even the courts have utilized these worldwide contracts to enlarge the extent of the basic liberties in the constitution of India. Therefore, it is feasible to judicially authorize an enormous number of basic liberties infringements epitomized in worldwide contracts moreover. However, the protected cum-global order should be joined by right friendly insights, support administrations and an essential change in family and cultural qualities. A legitimate implementation of these rights accordingly requires, instructing individuals in these basic liberties with the goal that these rights are regarded and seen by and by. A relieving society of common freedoms must be created in our country. Public Human Right Commission plays a larger part to play in managing cases and need to suggest and take compensatory measures. Individuals likewise need to mindful with regards to the commission and it is currently for individuals to take help of these accessible establishments to install basic liberties esteems in the home, locally, in the general public and in general society. Likewise, every one of the three mainstays of the public authority for example governing body, leader and legal executive should now regard and advance this culture of basic liberties uniquely for the ladies, the more fragile segment of the general public so that dealing with ladies and youngsters can be handled in a more noteworthy degree. Indeed, even the NGOs, government assistance organizations, legitimate specialists, common society and social laborers need to assume a significant part to get the privileges of the ladies, youngster through support, giving lawful guides and lawful training in the grass-root level to top.

GENDER EQUAL ALGORITHM – A POLICY PROPOSAL TOWARDS EQUALITY IN NEW AGE

Priyanka Vaidyanath
CHRIST (Deemed to be) University, India

Abstract

Gender equality seems to be a myth in the era of technology. Gender equality connotes equal consideration of genders in all domain, be it public or private. It's still astonishing how women's rights though considered as a human right is yet to be achieved. The fight for equality, equal consideration and equal opportunity seems to be poignant in the current day scenario. Passing by the days of hostility for 'equal pay for equal work', has landed women in no advantage but by bringing in newer ways of discrimination in today's world. The technologically advanced age is witnessing automation of activities thereby heavily relying on the Artificial Intelligence in public, professional and private sphere to take decisions mindlessly. The innate ability of the technology being biased is ignored intentionally (or not) by the entities using it. Artificial intelligence is where a machine: be it smart phones, computer, laptops or smart TV uses the data fed to classify, analyze and predict an outcome using algorithms. Algorithms utilize the data set to scrutinize patterns and behavior, thereby predicting an outcome or recommending suitable action/s. These predictions are improved automatically by experience and learning process of the system which is known as 'machine learning'. The need for the data set to be gender inclusive is pertinent owing to the use of AI in different realms of life and the way it learns and processes information. Artificial intelligence and machine learning is used by corporate entities, governmental organization and other corporate bodies in different areas influencing the social, economic and political structure of society. When the data that is fed into such AI machines are discriminatory against women, the algorithmic outcome leads to a biased prediction favoring men. The biased outcome affects women in employment, health care, education et al, leading to marginalizing the marginalized. According to World Economic Forum only 22% of AI professionals are female leading to imbalance and unequal representation of women which is alarming and reinforcing gender inequality. Thereby, to have a *'peaceful, prosperous and sustainable world'* (Agenda 5 of Sustainable Development Goals) before the clock ticks, a policy in place is quintessential.

Thus, the researcher presents a policy on having a gender equal algorithm to ensure gender equality in digital age with a special focus on marginalization of women. A qualitative method of research is adopted to collect data by imbibing doctrinal method of approach to analyze and interpret the data. There are primary and secondary data available in the form of scholarly literatures and statistical data by the world organizations (WEF, UNESCO) which shall be relied and utilized during the course of the research. The research aims to bring an impactful policy draft without limiting to any geographical space. The outcome of the policy is aimed at inclusiveness of all genders in the machine learning process thereby creating an equal sustainable world for all.

Introduction to Gender Equality

Gender equality is one of the Sustainable Development Goals (SDG) that the United Nations seek to reach at around 2035 which seems to be a realistic goal to many. "Gender Equality" as defined by the Oxford Dictionary means that the opportunities are not affected by the gender, that is the genders are seen equally without any preferential treatment. Though SDG advocate for gender equality, the pandemic has pushed the disparity to saddening state of affairs, wherein violence against women has increased, women work 2.5 hours more than men more so during the pandemic (Department of Economic and Social Affairs, 2021). The latest report by the World Economic Forum on the Gender Gap (World Economic Forum , 2021) states that 2021 has seen a 'step back' as against 2020 in terms of gender gap and takes nearly 135.6 years to neutralise the gap between the genders. Political empowerment, economic opportunities and participation have the largest gap while the gender gap has considerably reduced in education, health and survival (World Economic Forum , 2021). These facts and figures highlight the existing gender gap in the society in the 21st century also known to be as Modern Era.

Technology and Gender

The advanced science and technology owe a responsibility to the society to lead it into a sustainable equal world. While, the Artificial Intelligence, Machine Learning seems to negate the same, the activists believing in equality are advocating for algorithm equality before its late. Artificial intelligence (AI) has seen its presence in different sectors and the innovation continues each day to reach a better and finer place. The big companies like IBM, Apple, Microsoft, Facebook have been instrumental in bringing in change through AI even in a layman's life (Bernd W. Wirtz, 2019). AI is widely used in day-to-day life as well such as Face Lock on phones, smart assistants such as Siri and Alexa, personalised content on social media (Marr, 2019). AI is relied on by both public and private sector in terms of recruitment process wherein 47% of the US companies and 54% of jobs in European Union are computerised (Max Neufeind, 2018). In education which aims at empowering the students in self-learning, big tech companies such as Google and Microsoft are investing hugely to develop 'Artificial Intelligence in Education' (Wayne Holmes, 2019) Likewise, AI is extensively utilised in Agriculture, Healthcare, National security to ease the human pressure. There is no domain untouched by this recent advanced AI technology.

Having seen the widespread application of artificial intelligence, it seems imperative to understand what artificial intelligence is and how it works. Artificial intelligence is where the computer mimics or replicates a human behaviour in terms of 'human intelligence' (McCarthy, 2004). A machine needs to be guided for a specific outcome, so is the case with artificial intelligence. AI demands a step by step by guidance to think and further learns (Machine Learning) from the data fed into it (Stephen F Deangelis, 2014). Hence, artificial intelligence learns from the data fed into it and gives out probable outcomes for the situation put in, be it classifying job applications or any other kind of decision making. The decision-making process generally involves discrimination in various sense including gender, racial, religion and other. Discrimination in decision can occur due to inefficient labelling of data, lack of proper training on the data set, lack of generalised data and proxy data (Zuiderveen Borgesius, 2018). One such major discrimination thereby leading to bias is "Gender Bias" involved in the algorithm process consequently affecting the outcome. Gender bias or 'discrimination based on sex' is where there exists a prejudiced notion towards a gender more fully against women in terms of rights and dignity (Legal Information Institute, 2020).

It comes in as a surprise to believe that such advanced technology lacks in gender sensitisation and gender equality in its algorithm today. Regardless of the algorithm equality, gender inequality persists in its traditional senses as well. From childhood to adulthood girl children are prone to discrimination either at home or in the society. The world's women statistics highlights some of the discrimination that a woman faces (Department of Economic annd Social Affairs , 2020) wherein 28% of women hold managerial post globally, only 37 CEO among Fortune 500 companies. It is disturbing to come across gender inequality in advanced sciences as well. The pre-existing bias seems to be continued through algorithm bias wherein 22% of AI professionals are women as against 78% of men (World economic Forum , 2018). While the global index on the role of women in AI profession seems to be lower, the impact of gender bias imbibed in algorithm has a long-lasting affect in the domains it has been used.

These statistics showcases the need and importance to have gender inclusive data and here comes the role of the policy makers in putting in effort mindfully to ensure that such inclusion is seen since the early stages of the algorithmic growth and development. The goal 5 of the United Nation sustainable development goals (SDG) focuses on gender equality for *peaceful, prosperous and sustainable world'* which though not creates a legal obligation but is seen as a self-responsibility taken up by the governments with times update and review of the data collected in furtherance of the SDG (United Nations, 2016). The World Economic Forum took up a survey on the countries with the highest score in the performance level achieving SDG, Sweden topped with 84.5 followed by Denmark and Norway, wherein the list was dominated by the European countries (Willige, 2017). With apt policy in place, gender equality can be achieved.

It has already come into the UNESCO's attention about the gender inequality and artificial intelligence, where it has addressed issues concerning the in-built gender bias, to improve the role of women in technical domain and to create and have gender inclusive policies in place (UNESCO, 2020). Being aware of the existing inequality, inclusion of gender equality in artificial intelligence as one of the SDG can surely lead to proactive steps by the country.

Policy Recommendation with regard to coding of data set:

1. To have ethical principles about gender equality which is to be followed by the companies building AI software
2. The Big tech companies and Fortune 500 companies that are in the forefront in AI development to include equal representation of women in AI coding
3. To ensure that the data set are inclusive in nature
4. To have gender neutral tags while labelling the data
5. To feed in factually right and appropriate data sets to enhance machine learning in order to have positive impact on the society
6. To include the data sets that are in line with CEDAW and other Human Rights concerning women

Policy Recommendation with a view to create socio-economic equality through algorithm:

1. To encourage girl students to learn and involve in Science, Technology, Engineering and Mathematics (STEM) thereby breaking the stereotype
2. To make learning available in remote places and to students who cannot afford to go to school
3. To include women in managerial posts for equal representation and equal views on AI software development
4. To ensure that AI in public administration is well fed with gender equal data so as to have equal opportunities for women in grants and employment opportunities
5. To increase the virtual opportunities for women during times like pandemic in order to ensure that women do not fall behind in socio-economic status
6. To build AI software with an intention to govern and protect the privacy of all genders EQUALLY
7. To have gender neutral guidelines in classification of job applicants through AI
8. To ensure that search engines abide by gender neutral policies and exhibit non biased results

9. To remove sexist slurs and slang terms for women in search engines to create gender sensitivity
10. To include women specific health ailments to avoid wrong diagnosis during health check ups

Policy Recommendation in terms of cyber safety for women:

1. To build AI mechanism with the intention to track sexual offenders and the repetitive offenders thereby creating safe place for women
2. To sensitise and create awareness of vulnerability of women in virtual world
3. To have guidelines and limitations not to use and develop AI applications impairing the dignity of women on social media platforms
4. To detect and automatically delete offensive languages, lured comments
5. To develop AI chatbots to help victims to share and support them during crisis
6. To offer continuous psychological support to victims of sexual abuse and assault

With the back drop of achieving sustainable development goals, nation states have to involve in research and development of AI to be gender inclusive in both public and private sectors. Owing to the lack of clarity with regard to responsibility being attached to the wrong doings and mis doings of AI, the national governing bodies can set up a redressal mechanism to look into case-by-case basis of fault / violation of rights aided by AI. Without having an enforcement mechanism no policy or law can regulate the disparity. The burden also falls on the developer in terms of social responsibility to instil confidence amongst genders to create an inclusive society.

It better now than never, therefore, we have to thrive and seek that the algorithms are correctly guided to include gender equal data sets before it causes irreparable damage on the society.

References

Bernd W. Wirtz, J. C. (2019). Artificial Intelligence and the Public Sector—Applications and Challenges. *International Journal of PUblic Administration* , 569-615.

Department of Economic and Social Affairs, S. D. (2021). *Achieve gender equality and empower all women and girls.* United Nation. Retrieved from https://sdgs.un.org/goals/goal5

Department of Economic annd Social Affairs . (2020). *The World's Women 2020 : Trends and Statistics.* United Nation .

Legal Information Institute. (2020). *Gender Bias* . Retrieved from Cornell Law School : https://www.law.cornell.edu/wex/gender_bias

Marr, B. (2019, December 19). *The 10 Best Examples Of How AI Is Already Used In Our Everyday Life.* Retrieved from Forbes: https://www.forbes.com/sites/bernardmarr/2019/12/16/the-10-best-examples-of-how-ai-is-already-used-in-our-everyday-life/?sh=758989221171

Max Neufeind, J. O. (2018). *Work in the Digital Age: Challenges of the fourth Industrial Revolution.* Rowman & Littlefield International Ltd.

McCarthy, J. (2004, November). What is Artificial Intelligence? Stanford , California , United States of America .

Stephen F Deangelis, S. (2014, September). *Artificial Intelligence: How Algorithms Make Systems Smart.* Retrieved from Wired: https://www.wired.com/insights/2014/09/artificial-intelligence-algorithms-2/

UNESCO. (2020). *Artificial Intelligence and Gender Equality.* Paris: UNESCO.

United Nations. (2016). *The Sustainable Development Agenda.* Retrieved from United Nations: https://www.un.org/sustainabledevelopment/development-agenda-retired/

Wayne Holmes, M. B. (2019). *Artificial Intelligence in Education.* Massachusetts: The Center for Curriculum Redesign.

Willige, A. (2017, March 20). *Which countries are achieving the UN Sustainable Development Goals fastest?* Retrieved from WOrld Economic Forum: https://www.weforum.org/agenda/2017/03/countries-achieving-un-sustainable-development-goals-fastest/

World economic Forum . (2018). *Assessing Gender Gaps in Artificial Intelligence.* World Economic Forum.

World Economic Forum . (2021). *Global Gender Gap Report 2021.* Geneva: World Economic Forum.

Zuiderveen Borgesius, F. (2018). *Discrimination, artificial intelligence, and algorithmic decision-making.* Amsterdam: Council of Europe, Directorate General of Democracy.

ENHANCING PARTICIPATION OF YOUTH TO IMPRIOVE EDUCATION QUALITY IN RURAL AREAS: THE CASE OF KOTA BELUD, SABAH, MALAYSIA

Zuraidah Mohd Amin
University of Malaya, Malaysia

Abstract

Education quality among youth who lived in rural areas has become a prolonged issue, especially across developing countries. Limitation of getting excellent access to education becomes part of challenges to create a better quality of education among youth. As a result, youth who stayed in rural areas not be able to compete with other youths around the world in the future.

Kota Belud is one of the districts located on the west coast of Sabah state, Malaysia. Kota Belud has become the focused area of the policy to enhance youth participation to create a better education quality. The participation of youth at the international level is also very less due to limited access to sources of information, and limited facilities available in education institutions. Therefore, the chances of youth participating at the international level are very limited.

Therefore, by having bilateral cooperation from the local Ministry of Education and international youth associations, the participation of youth can increase so that the objective in improving education quality for a better future. International youth associations should take this opportunity to create a platform and connect youth from international territories with youth from Kota Belud. Bilateral cooperation from these key players becomes a bridge to connect with youths in Kota Belud with youths around the world to gain a real experience directly.

International youth associations are also able to conduct exchange programs with youth in Kota Belud with international youth to exchange and ideas and experiences. The programs can widen the eyes of youths to celebrate the differences among youths around the world. At the same time, youth in Kota Belud is also able to improve their communication skills, increase youth confidence level, and able to promote local culture experience as well.

The action by having a collaboration of international youth associations with the local ministry of Education can also replicate in another location around the world. As long as the focused group should be located in a rural area to ensure youth who lived in the rural area able to get access to create a better quality education parallel with the 4th of Sustainable Development Goals (SDG) in improving quality education and the 17th of SDG which highlighting about the Partnerships for the Goals.

Introduction

Education is one amongst the crucial elements that ought to be prioritized so as to shape a decent quality of youth for an improved future. Youth become the most group of a generation who exposed to current development and therefore the encouragement to explore the globe is required as youth would be part of the active labour market. Thus, identification of age range is needed so that local state actors are able to plan for development programs specialized for youth. In the case of Malaysia, the range of youth in Malaysia catered from 15 until 40 years old. However, in order to focus on shaping youth development program specified only in the range of 18 until 25 years old. (National Youth Development Policy, 1997).

Meanwhile, the youth usually spends teenage years from 15-18 years old in secondary schools and utilizing the range age from 19-25 years old to pursue tertiary education. The time-frame as per illustrated is needed to identify the crucial years for youth. Thus, the ten years are crucial for state actors developing any youth development program as that specific period ought to be utilized to adequate with knowledge and various range of skil
l sets as preparation before entering challenging career world.
Nevertheless, youth in Kota Belud, Sabah is facing difficulties to obtain a good quality of education. The situation has become a prolonged issue since Malaysia achieved independence back in 1957. The development in every state is varied lead unbalance in development across the states within Malaysia. Thus, the rural regions also received an impact that impacting youth to receive formal education from formal institutions. The number of youth to complete

94

their schooling in secondary school also in a low rate. Based on research conducted by Tangit *et al* (2014), 54.2% of 378 respondents obtained secondary education as the highest education. But, only 6.1% received and completed tertiary education in degree. Even though the research has been conducted nearby Kota Belud and the significance of the situation able clearly illustrate from previous research. The situation creates pressure towards youth to compete with other youth around the world when they start their journey in career as the level of competition at the international stage is much competitive.

Therefore, this paper leads to the method in enhancing the participation of youth to improve education quality by focusing on youth concentrated in Kota Belud, Sabah. The analysis of policy paper will cover the background of the current education situation in Sabah as an overview of the current condition before providing the primary suggestion of the method that should be implemented by state actors followed by the alternative proposal in order to improve the education quality among youth in Kota Belud, Sabah.

Problem Description

The lack of number of a formal institutions in Kota Belud, drives the low rate of literacy and the youth face difficulties in surviving in labour market. Tangit, *et al* (2014) also highlighting about the literary and the level of education received among the respondents nearby Kota Belud is still less encouraging as only 54.2% of respondents had received formal education until secondary school. In fact, the figure of respondents who have not received any formal education is beyond 5% but less than 10%.

Thus, how is the quality of education among youth able to improve even though they are lived in such far from urban development, less equipped with advanced technologies? The question kept on arising, especially if I look at the education issue across developing countries. The gap in order to obtain the right to education should have not become one of the major issues in a developing country like Malaysia. Thus, the situation is supposed to manage and improve as much as the government should. The target of United Nations Sustainable Development Goals should be realized in order to improve education quality as highlighted in the 4th SDG.

In order for the youth to be able to compete with other youth around the world, the youth need to be adequate with a sufficient set of skills to survive and be able to be compete with others. Therefore, suitable alternatives proposals would be identified. In addition, the critical analysis also would be defined to determine the effective action that needs to be taken by the government to encounter the prolonged issue in the development of education in Malaysia.

Policy Options

The SDG has highlighted the importance of improving education quality and partnerships are also needed in achieving the SDG goals. Thus, improving education quality in Kota Belud, Sabah also linked in order to ensure the 4th goal in SDG able to be achieved and the local government should revisit two options in order to improve education and enhance the participation of youth into the international arena:

Increase the formal institutions within the rural areas

Kota Belud is one of the districts in Sabah which has a lesser number of secondary schools compare with the primary schools in Kota Belud. As per data in 2016, there are 45 primary schools and 12 primary schools located in remote areas. Meanwhile, only 9 secondary schools exist in Kota Belud. Such a huge gap of number formal institutions exists in Kota Belud, which create the instability in getting formal education and completing study until secondary school. (Information Management Unit, 2016).

However, increasing the number of formal institutions in Kota Belud does not guarantee to lead the effectiveness of creating good quality in education. Besides no solid evidence is there, to prove the level of effectiveness in creating an excellent quality in education if the government increasing the number of formal institutions. In fact, the cost required and to be included in the annual national budget also would be increased as well. Besides, the government also needs to consider and allocate extra budget if needed to build formal institutions in a rural region. The increasing allocation in budget is needed due to the additional cost that needs to be borne by the government as to get access and bring the materials required to build a school in a mountainous terrain surrounding the Kota Belud.

Due to geographical factors, access to the internet and network also become part of obstacles to shape a better quality in education especially in the Kota Belud district. Even though internet connection exists in the Kota Belud region, however, the range of connections is still in moderate coverage. In fact, the physical condition leads the burnout towards teaching staff as well because based on research conducted by Rathakrishnan *et al* (2020), concluded that significant value exists between teaching staff who are allocated between rural and urban areas of Sabah state whereby the decreasing feeling of self-achievement among teaching staff for a rural area more significant compared to those teaching staff in an urban area.

Encourage the collaboration with international youth associations

Marwan *et al* (2012) highlighted one interesting finding in the context of education in rural areas whereby the biggest part of the problem in rural education was a limitation in English competency among youth as several pieces of researches have been done by several scholars in teaching the English language in the rural region around Malaysia. The current situation in rural education is also stressed by Azman (2006), whereby the ethnographic has become a contributing factor of the cause of lacking literacy in English in the rural regions. Ler (2012), also supported the culture attached affecting the English literacy among youth concentrated in the rural regions besides lack of English speaking environment in daily life. The norms and standard language which was practiced since childhood without much exposure to international language, created a pressure among the youth once they jumped into career world, especially to compete with the youth from urban areas or international level.

Therefore, a series of improving English skills among youth was introduced across the rural regions in Malaysia. Asraf and Ahmad (2003) stressed the ability in the English language among students and reviewed the success of the GER (Guided Extensive Reading) program, upon four-months of having programs in the rural region in different locations in Malaysia. Palmer and Atiqah (2008), also replicated the similar idea in improving the ability of youth by having a program called Project to Improve English in Rural Schools (PIERS). The success of improving English skills has been spread up until Sabah, as the cooperate level also sponsored the program to help the Non-Governmental Organization (NGO) in running the program (Borneo Post, 2012).

Nevertheless, there are limitations of youth participation at the international level due to the programs being limited to the national level even though the objective of the English program is to improve the English skills among youth. Thus, the range of networks among youth is still limited in specific regions and stacked at the national level. The diversity of knowledge and exposure from youth towards the international level is also limited. The encouragement of youth to speak with the native speakers is also limited, as they are speaking to their friends who natively speak in local-Malaysia language.

Therefore, having collaborations with international youth associations from the international level is necessary to expand the range of networking as a preparation part for youth, to involve in the international segments. Besides improving English skills, they are able to exchange cultural experiences with youth from around the world. Thus, the diversity of culture is able to learn and be adaptive among the youth. The bandwidth of network among youth shall expand and increase the confidence level in communication. by talking with English native speakers as well.

Thus, the local government and local state actors encourage to have a collaboration with the international youth associations to enhance the youth participation. Besides, local state actor entities such as the Ministry of Youth and Sports are also able to become part of linkages towards international youth associations to accelerate the program into specific areas in Kota Belud. The connection between local entities is able to encourage the networking across functions, so that the promotion of the program is able to expand as well.

Series of a program must be designed by international youth association, should also diversify in terms of achieving a goal in order to improve English skills among local people because of the local youth will have a great chance to communicate directly with native speakers, besides being able to learn various English slangs, around the world. This is to ensure that, they are able to adapt with the slang even though the English words are the same but drive a different sound. The chances would be beneficial towards the youth as the exposure of confidently speaking, outside their circle is able to improve from time to time. As a result, the opportunity among them to expand their knowledge is higher than interacting among in the same circle of communities.

Exchanging thoughts and ideas, also become part of the outcome from the program designed by international youth association. As the participant will be interacting with other participants from an international youth, they would be able to learn the culture and exchange their ideas and thoughts, with other participants. This is where creative and critical thinking comes from. Because to have a different idea would be great in order to be a comparative person and diplomatic person. Besides, the participants were also able to celebrate the differences in culture that exist around in the world, because the participants are from various backgrounds around the world.

Besides, having a program with an international youth association which has English as a medium, the transferable skills also become part of the slot program which international youth associations must include in their program. The demanding skills such as Information Technology (IT), become common demanding skills needed in the job market. Thus, programs such as entrepreneurship through e-commerce become a good platform for youth. Besides improving education quality, they are able to prepare themselves for the international labour market. The prospect of a job in the future needs to be analytical, besides possessing expertise in utilizing the technologies as the world is moving towards an Industrial Revolution 4.0, whereby the complexity of the system and technologies are able to ease human daily activities. Hence, the youth need to be adequate with sufficient skill set to ensure that the youth in Kota Belud, are able to compete with other youth in the international platform. (Zahidi *et al*, 2020)

Conclusion and Recommendation

The option of having collaboration with local state actors such as the local Ministry of Education and Ministry of Youth and Sports, have become a catalyst in enhancing the participation of youth in the international arena and shaping a better education quality in the future. Research has been conducted to measure the effectiveness of having a program in improving education quality. Nevertheless, the exposure and implementation towards the international level are still in the low range. Thus, having a collaboration between local entities and international youth associations would be beneficial towards youth especially those living in rural areas and have limited access to a proper education.

On other hand, adding a huge budget to build formal institutions somehow did not ensure the effectiveness of improving education quality as it would be, increasing the operation cost without measuring the level of effectiveness. In fact, having collaboration with international youth associations is capable of lowering the overall operation cost in improving education quality activities. Ultimately, having such a great collaboration between local state actors and international youth associations, was able to spur the great impact towards youth around Kota Belud, Sabah.

Nevertheless, there are limitations due to COVID 19 pandemic, which restrict the movement of people around the world. Even though there are possibilities of having a collaboration with youth or local state actors to launch the projects via a virtual or online platform, in order to execute the programme, one needs to look at the basic physical infrastructure and limitations in the project location. The virtual session or online learning session needs to have good internet coverage. The obstacle in terms of having a better coverage of internet, needs to be taken care by the local state actors. Otherwise, the collaborators would be able to start round-table discussions with local state actors and launch the projects upon the world getting better. In another around, the local state actors were also able to revisit in order to improve the internet coverage in the rural areas, before launching the project with international youth associations.

The feature of having a collaboration is also able to replicate to another location in the developing or less developing countries around the world. The hidden idea of having partnerships with international youth associations, is to ensure there is mobility to move, flexibility, and a vision to improve, the education quality for benefits towards future generations. Besides, the projection of outcome is able to measure the changes and improvement among the youth or vice versa, within three to five years upon completion of the program. Therefore, a follow up on the progress of participants or youth also might be needed as testimony before replicating the program to another location around the world.

In a nutshell, the consideration and the success of the partnership between local state actors and international youth associations are able to consider it as a part of the annual project at the national and international level to ensure the objective of having SDG goals, which are to be completed.

Bibliography

Asraf, R. M., & Ahmad, I. S. (2003). Promoting English language development and the reading habit among   students   in   rural schools through the Guided Extensive Reading program. Reading in a Foreign   Language, 15(2). ISSN: 1539-0578

Azman, H. (2006). English language in rural Malaysia: situating global literacies in local practices. 3L: Language, Linguistics, Literature. The Southeast Asian Journal of English Language Studies, 11, 99-   119

Borneo Post (2012). HSBC and Hap Seng-sponsored PIERS lifts English education in Sabah. 5 April 2012. Retrieved   from: https://www.theborneopost.com/2012/04/05/hsbc-and-hap-seng-sponsored-piers-lifts- english-education-in-sabah/

Information Management Unit. (2016). List of primary schools in Sabah according to category: Rural areas and remote   areas. Sabah Education Department, Kota Kinabalu Sabah.

Lee, E. C. (2012). Cultural Factor Affecting English Proficiency in Rural Area. Advances in Language and   Literacy   Studies. Australian International   Academic   Centre,   Australia.   3(1). doi:10.7575/aiac.alls.v.3n.1p.1

Marwan, A., Sumintono, B., & Mislan, N. (2012). Revitalizing Rural Schools: A Challenge for Malaysia.   Educational Issues, Research and Policies. In Chapter: Revitalizing Rural Schools: A Challenge for Malaysia. 172-188. UTM Press RMC

National Youth Development Policy. (1997). Ministry of Youth and Sports Malaysia. Division of Youth   Development. Putrajaya.

Palmer, S. & Atiqah (2008). Project to Improve English in Rural Schools (PIERS), Jelebu Pertang, Negeri   Sembilan. CfBT Education Malaysia. Available at: www.cfbt.com.my/PIERS Jelebu Pertang Final   Report.pdf

Rathakrishnan, B., George, S., Singh, S. S. B., Kamaludin, M. R., & Wani, M. A. (2020). Burnout among   Secondary School Teachers in Malaysia Sabah. Journal of Xidian University, 14 (4). ISSN 1001-2400.

Tangit, T. M., Hasim, A. K. M. H., & Rural, A. A. (2014). Tourism at its Peak: Socio-Cultural Impacts towards Host Communities of Kinabalu Park, Sabah (Malaysian Borneo). SHS Web of Conferences 12. EDP Sciences 2014. DOI: 10.1051/shsconf/20141201097

Zahidi, S., Racheva. V., Hingel, G., Brown., S. (2020). The Future Job Report 2020. World Economic Forum.   Geeneva, Switzerland. October 2020.

THE WAR ON RIFGHTS: RESTRICTIONS ON HUMAN RIGHTS IN THE CNTEXT OF THE STATE OF A HEALTH EMERGENCY IN THE DEMOCRATIC REPUBLIC OF CONGO

Richard Lumbika
Me Ninon Muanda Mbuangi

Introduction

Our dignity is not negotiable; our children need love and not masks," Dutch people chanted on Sunday, January 24, 2021. They were protesting the restrictive measures taken to deal with the second wave of covid-19. Three nights of rioting! This reminds us of Kinshasa[162]: people lost their lives when demonstrators demanded the reopening of the central market, which had been closed since the end of March 2020[163] After the Gombe commune was locked down.

Executive order No. 20/014 of March 24, 2020, declaring the state of health emergency in the Democratic Republic of Congo, clearly restrict some rights and freedoms. These include the prohibition of meetings and celebrations of more than twenty people in public places; schools, universities, and colleges were closed; the suspension of places of worship, sports activities, discotheques, bar-cafés, terraces, restaurants, and funeral homes. Flights from countries at risk have been suspended, except for cargo planes and ships and other means of transport. Trips to the Democratic Republic of Congo from countries at risk have been postponed, whereas passengers arriving in Congo are required to fill in an information sheet, wash their hands, undergo temperature sampling, and a quarantine for any suspected person. Controls are reinforced at all entry posts and in the movement of people from Kinshasa to other provinces of the country.

The state of a health emergency is declared in order to safeguard the

---

[162] A lockdown has been declared. The Covid-19 response team "will be organized to search for sick people, but also to investigate contacts at risk and symptomatic cases throughout the city of Kinshasa for their screening and treatment" cfr Ouest-France.fr/sante/virus/coronavirus/ consulted on January 27, 2021, 09: 01
[163] Agence Belga, June 9, 2020, 23:44.

right to health, and more globally, the right to life. The rules imposed are highly restrictive of civil, political, economic, social, or cultural human rights. The free movement of persons, which is fundamental to economic activity, especially in the context of poverty, is limited. Therefore, there is a conflict between the rights that are intended to be protected and the rights that are restricted. A war of rights, whereas human rights are meant to be interdependent, as they are indivisible as much as their holder: the human being.

Freedom of movement is subject to restrictions in the name of the right to health. If the measure is neutral and impersonal, it is imposed on people in different situations. This could result in indirect discrimination, indirect cumulative violations, cascading violations of human rights. Freedom of movement has significant consequences where informal activity is a source of life or survival. There is, therefore, a real conflict between the right to health, which is the subject of health emergency measures, and freedom of movement, without which access to resources is not possible. Can one of these rights be limited to the benefit of the other? Which right will be prioritized over the other? Should there be a hierarchy of rights?

After recalling the theory of the indivisibility of human rights (1), this paper will posit the right to life as a right to survival (2), requiring the effectiveness of free movement (3). Their limitation in the context of the state of emergency in the Democratic Republic of Congo should be justified (4), while the rights-based approach seems appropriate to reduce the effects of the "rights war" (5).

The theory of indivisibility and interdependence of human rights

The archipelago of human rights[164] Offers a real indivisibility that it is no longer relevant to classify them into generations, insofar as interaction relationships unite them, despite their successive establishment in the philosophy of generations. Civil and political rights, the first generation, are found in the declarations of the 18th century. Economic, social, and cultural rights, the second generation, was

---

[164] P.GERARD, The spirit of rights. Philosophy of Human Rights, Larcier, Brussels, 2017,
p. 31 and following.

known, following certain constitutions, by the Universal Declaration of Human Rights (art. 22 to 27). The collective rights of the third generation, among which are counted the right to development, the right to peace, the right to the environment, are enshrined in various statements.

This typology is outdated based on an analysis of the corresponding human rights obligations. Indeed, it is evident that the negative obligations or abstention incumbent on governments are not the only ones imposed by civil and political rights. Likewise, economic, social, and cultural rights do not require only positive obligations. Civil and political rights entail both negative and positive obligations for the public authorities, as much for the rights of the second generation.[165].

Consider the right to life, the right to health, and the right to a healthy environment. in addition to the obligation to refrain, the government must take positive steps to prevent the violation of this right and take measures to promote and protect life. The right to health requires the government to take steps towards its realization and refrain from any policy that impedes that right. The right to a healthy environment requires the government to take positive measures to protect and promote it and refrain from any tangible or intangible act that may impede the effectiveness of that right. The right to life can only be realized if the right to health is effective, all in a healthy environment. There is, therefore, interdependence and indivisibility of human rights. This is not surprising when we know that all these rights have the same holder: the human being.

The indivisibility and interdependence of these rights is found in the request of the President to the Constitutional Court; <<thus, the Court ruled that executive order No. 20/014 of March 24, 2020, complies with the Constitution and guarantees the right provided for in Article 47, paragraph 1 of the Constitution as well as the right for all persons to a healthy environment conducive to integral development as set out in Article 1er the Constitution>>[166]

The protection of health and life are legitimate objectives of the limi-

---

[165] Ibid, p. 32
[166] R.CONST 1.200

tation of rights and freedoms and positive obligations for governments. The same thing applies to the protection and preservation of
the environment. Are they not, therefore, caught between the ham-
mer and the anvil?

The right to survival/life in the freedom of movement

A. **Life and survival through the informal sector**

The right to life in disadvantaged environments is, first and fore-
most, a right to survival. Following René Dumont, it is appropriate
to affirm that "the first right of a human being (is) that of satisfying
his or her essential needs, and first of all those which ensure survival:
the right to eat properly and to have access to drinking water."[167].

The riots in Tripoli, the week of January 24, 2021, with the scream
"Feed us and give us to drink, and we will leave the streets."[168], like
the blunder of the vendors of the big market in Kinshasa, reveal the
economic insecurity, which is covered only by daily survival capacities, therefore calling for freedom of movement that the measures to
fight the pandemic have come to restrict.

"The daily hunger, the daily distress, is, by its repetition, much less
spectacular[169]. It is devastating, but it is not as broadcasted as famine.
"Decent housing is also an element of survival because men and
women do not live on bread alone: they have a right to dignity and
respect[170]. "Survival (...) depends on a social reflex that experts (...)
try to tame by talking about the informal sector or civil society[171].

Public sector jobs do not necessarily protect against survival mechanisms. Low wages have given rise to a 'parallel business logic'. This
logic mobilizes the indigenous in the daily struggle for survival from
the bottom up. This struggle can be summed up in one major imperative: to find food (understood not only as a daily ration but also

---

[167] R. DUMONT, Democracy for Africa, Paris, Seuil, 1991, p.240.
[168] Newspaper of January 29, 2021, 21h00, France 24
[169] R.DUMONT, p.240
[170] R.DUMONT p.242
[171] J.-M. ELA, Africa. The irruption of the poor. Society against interference,
power and money, Paris, L Harmattan, 1994, p. 62.

as investments in small sectors that can substantially remove the specter of starvation and leave a legacy for one's family)[172]. "The majority of African women must learn to manage in the various sectors of small-scale market production: small retail shops, crafts, sewing workshops, makeshift restaurants in the streets. This microbusiness provides additional income for the family, for which women often assume all the burden."[173].

Indeed, one should not minimize the survival capacity in activities such as auction sales, rickshawing, pottering, pavement sales, the occasional bar under trees, car washing, hairdressing...All these activities require energy and good health. Staying at home means exposing oneself to death, life is "day by day", like these "small restaurant called *Malewas*, these small makeshift restaurants where people are served a plate of local dishes quickly and for a few."[174] a kind of right to survival is the slogan of the people who have to go out every day in search of bread for their families. There is a right to survival. "The survival of many men and women depends on a social reflex that the experts ...try to tame by talking about the informal sector.[175]. The right to survival cannot, therefore, be conceived in the context of poor health. There is a clear interdependence between the right to health and the right to life.

B. **The right to health**
C.

The right to health is a right of claim. It calls for public service and regulatory service obligations. First, the government provides services through the public hospital and ensures access to these services. Second, the regulatory service is reflected in the regulation of the healthprofessions in order to guarantee the quality of care, the quantity of health care facilities, and the control of pharmacies. This includes rules such as the prohibition of dumping trashanywhere, the prohibition to smoke in certain places. Furthermore, it includes obligations such as village sanitation, barrier gestures, wearing of

---

[172] A. MBEMBE, Indocile Africa. Christianity, power and the state in postcolonial society, Paris, Kathala, 1988, p. 165
[173] J.-M. ELA, op.cit, p.91
[174] DJUNGU-SIMBA K, La mangeoire, Les Editions du Pangolin, Enghien, 2017, p.13.
[175] *Ibid*

masks, hand washing, social distancing, mandatory vaccinations...
These measures could upset or restrict other rights such as freedom
of trade and industry, freedom of choice of treatment, freedom of
consent to vaccination...[176]

The Covid-19 pandemic is global. It is true that it started in Wuhan,
China, but crisis management is a challenge for the poor in poor
countries. Access to the vaccine raises concerns: South Africa and
India have proposed to the WTO to lift intellectual property rights,
the European Union, champion of human rights, has opposed. The
rich prioritize vaccinating their own populations. The vaccine nationalism shown by rich countries reveals the fracture of humanity.
Yet to contain the pandemic in one's own country without concern
for neighbors, as well as distant partners, is to go the wrong way. An
outbreak in one country remains a danger for the whole planet.
Thus, the legend of the lizard and the grass-snake takes its meaning.

She *said that a snake and a lizard were arguing on an old woman's
roof. Both appealed to the old woman as a referee. The old woman
refused. They sought the mediation of a horse next door, and then an
ox, who refused in turn. When the dispute reached a climax, a fight
broke out. The two reptiles fell on the old woman'sfire. The hut caught
fire. A young man took the horse to go to the village for help and ran
so fast that the horse died. And when help came, the old woman was
dead.She was buried and the ox was grilled for memorial services.*

Environmental and health security are indivisible, as the globalization of the coronavirus demonstrates. If the solutions to the problem
are reduced to the limited space of the rich, the problem may remain. Indeed, it is shameful to be happy when others are in misery.
The WHO Director-General Tedros Adhanaon Ghebreyesus warns
against vaccine nationalism, especially in view of the European Union's all-out vaccination drive, doubling itspre-orders of Pfizer's an-
ti-Covid vaccine _ BioNTech. Covax is set up by the WHO and the
Global Alliance for Vaccines and Immunization (GAVI) to distribute
Covid vaccines to poor countries. Contracts for two billion vaccines

---

[176] T. GRÜNDLER, " Effectiveness, effectiveness, efficiency. The example of
the right to health ", in V. CHAMPEIL-DESPLATS, D. LOCHAK, A the search
for the effectiveness of human rights, Paris, Presses universitaires de Paris
10, 2008, p. 33.

to be deployed after delivery[177].The world has reached a critical juncture in the Covid-19 pandemic," said the UN agency's DG. But also, a turning point in history; in the face of a common crisis, can nations come together in a common approach?[178]Likewise, Speaking at the Davos summit, Cyril Ramaphosa, President of RSA, stressed: "We are not all safe if some countries vaccinate their populations and others do not. We must all act together to fight the coronavirus because it affects us all in the same way".[179]

Ultimately, when the neighbor's hut is burning, it is better to help him and put out the firebecause it can reach one's home.

Freedom of movement, pivotal freedom for health and life

The freedom of movement can be divided into three rights:

- o fundamental freedom is exercised without prior authorization or declaration.Article 12 of the PDCP states that "anyone who is lawfully within the territory of a country has the right to move about freely ."The Congolese law and international law guarantee the exercise of freedom of movement on the Congolese territory for both Congolese and foreigners, provided that the latter comply with the law and regulation on foreigners. It is legitimate for a country to subject the free movement of foreigners to restrictive conditions to regulate the entry, stay, and removal of foreigners.
- o The freedom of movement within a territory includes, in addition, the right to leave that territory. "Everyone is free to leave any country, including his or her own," according to Article 12 of the PDCP.
- o Freedom of movement gives the right to enter one's own country from abroad; "No one shall be deprived of the right to enter the territory of the country of which he is a national. "This is an absolute right because, unlike the previous two, it cannot be waived.

This goes without saying that measures taken by executive order

---

[177] AFP, Dispatch of January 8 2021
[178] *ibid*
[179] En. africanews.com/2021/01

No. 20/01 of March 24 declaring a state of health emergency to deal with the Covid-19 pandemic are highly restrictive of freedom of movement. That is the case when the country closes its borders to passengers and any person, the suspension of all flights from countries at risk and transit countries.[180]. The prohibition of all kinds of trips from Kinshasa to provinces and from provincesto Kinshasa, the epicenter of the pandemic, with the ultimate aim of locking down the capital[181]. Restriction of freedom of movement, in the context of the right to survival, is possible through the ability to move of informal entrepreneurs and consumers of services.

Indeed, if the mobile for these restrictions is to contain the pandemic "which, by its nature and gravity, endangers the health of people."[182], it is because these restrictions are aimed at protecting the life and health of people, which are not possible without theoutcome of entrepreneurial and informal mobility. So, there is a dilemma: let people go for the right to survival during the pandemic, lockdown people, and let them starve. "Stay at home, I starve.Go out, I eventually die of covid. I go out, and God will provide[183].

For informal workers, the restriction of free movement was as much a disaster as the coronavirus.In a search for balance, "the Congolese government should take into account not only the health of its people but also all their rights (...), develop, with its local and international partners, strategies to assist the most vulnerable populations and ensure that health professionals work in a safe manner," Human Rights Watch believes.[184].

Coming and going goes beyond the law to become part of human life as an imperative. Life iscelebrated and moves to the rhythm of steps. Economic activity, both formal and informal, cannot go without this freedom. Indeed, it is a matter of "moving", as soon as one is up, on foot or by means of locomotion, to produce, pray, study, and be cared for... As much as moving sets free from the place of departure, it also binds one to the place of destination, of realization. moving

---

[180] Article 2 of Order No. 20/014 of March 24, 2020
[181] Article 3 of Order No. 20/014 of March 24, 2020
[182] Article 1 of Order No. 20/014 of March 24, 2020
[183] Words from a lime worker
[184] Hrw.org/en/news/2010/04/rd_Congo

sets free[185], and the lockdown imprisons.

In daily urban and village life, life is celebrated in beer and prayer[186]. Places and occasions for meeting and gathering, which the health emergency measures have literally shut down, at the same time highlighting their significance in urban life. A Congolese novelist's picture of beer and its accompaniments is sufficiently elucidating. Let's listen to him: "The sun, the heat,the week that has to be paid for with shouts, music and dances, with the fumes and smells of all the over-spiced meats (...), these meats that are grilled over smoldering embers and swallowedwith hectoliters of alcohol in order to stay on their feet until the wee hours of the morning... And to boost all of this fauna, the masanga-pump! We can never thank enough, in this city, in this country, the Belgian colonists and nokos who invented and bequeathed to their Congolese wards this nectar called beer which concentrates in it all the virtues of independence and atmosphere.

Freedom of religion! Churches are places of meeting daily. The word of God is preached and nourishes the hope of believers.[187]. Daily prayer gatherings are made up of trance rituals, believers praying aloud, speaking in tongues, pastors casting out demons.[188]. In terms of beliefs and practices, Africa remains a deeply religious continent. The Democratic Republic of Congo has experienced a real religious awakening in recent years, marked by a continuously growing number of churches... Most believers expect religion to solve their daily existential problems, especially in a socio-economic context marked by economic crises'[189].

If the practice of faith is a solution to everyday problems, the fight against the pandemic shouldmobilize people in prayer. The suspension of places of worship[190], despite the secular nature of the state, it

---

[185] F. GROS, Walking, a philosophy, Paris, Carnets Nord, 2009, p.11

[186] D.VAN REYBROUCK, Congo. A History, Amsterdam, Actes Sud, 2012, p. 497 ff.

[187] J.-M. ELA, Ma foi d'africain, Paris, Karthala, 1985, p. 17

[188] D. VAN REYBROUCK, op. cit. pp. 526-527

[189] TELOMONO BISANGAMANI, 'Right to pray or right to cry out in the DRC? Remarks by a Christian jurist on the illegality of prayer ", in Annales juridique africaines, Vol. II, N ° 1, September 2020, p. 1982.

[190] Article 3.4 of the Ordinance

is seen as a violation of the right to religious freedom. Indeed, it is a right for every person to choose and express his or her faith (freedom of conscience), but also to engage in rites and practices related to faith (freedom of worship): "Everyone has the right to freedom of thought, conscience, and religion.[191]". Hence, can we forbid worship to people who consider that salvation from the pandemic lies in prayer? The question also arises with regard to the prohibition of funeral vigils, when we know that "the cult of the dead is perhaps the cultural aspect to which Africans feel most attached; ...represents a heritage that is valued above all else"[192]. As Birago Diop writes, the dead are not dead!

Therefore, it is necessary to examine the conditions under which limitations of rights are possible.

Justification of restrictions on human rights

Restrictions on rights are permitted under certain conditions. The instruments for the protection of human rights set three conditions: respect for the principle of legality, the legitimacy of the aim pursued, and the need for restriction in a democratic society[193]. The principle of legality requires that the restriction has a basis in the domestic law of the country. The aim is to protect against arbitrariness and comply with the rule of law as required by all human rights protection systems. Indeed, the authority restricting rights must do so within its competence. The PDCP, in relation to freedom of movement and freedom to manifest one's religion, states that restrictions must be provided by law.

Restrictions on rights must have a legitimate objective, that is, to protect values that are important in order to limit the enjoyment or exercise of human rights[194]. The Syracuse Principles have public order, national security, public safety, public health, public morals,

---

[191] Article 22 of the 2006 Constitution
[192] J.-M. ELA, op.cit. p. 36.
[193] L.HENNEBEL, H. TIGROUDJA, Treaty of international human rights law, 2nd edition, Paris, A. Pedone, p. 699
[194] Idem, p. 700

and the rights of others as legitimate objectives[195]. These circumstances may be combined and include, for example, "the protection of public safety, order, and health, or morals or the rights and freedoms of others."[196]. In the case of the Covid-19 pandemic, public health is at stake: it constitutes a serious threat to the health of the Congolese population and the global human community.

Finally, the restrictions must be necessary. Necessity assesses the reasonableness of the restrictions and thus their proportionality. Indeed, they "must be appropriate to fulfill their protective function, they must be the least disruptive of the means that could achieve the desired result, and they must be proportionate to the interest to be protected", notes the United Nations Human Rights Committee[197]. The Congolese ConstitutionConstitution excludes, even in a proclaimed state of emergency, derogation from the following fundamental rights and principles: "1. the right tolife; 2. the prohibition of torture and cruel, inhuman or degrading treatment or punishment; 3. the prohibition of slavery and servitude; 4. The principle of the legality of criminal offenses and penalties; Rights of defense and the right to appeal; 6. Prohibition of imprisonment for debt; 7. Freedomof thought, conscience, and religion[198].

The state of health emergency in the DRC seems to have limited freedom of worship, a fundamental dimension of religious freedom. Should this be seen as a breach of the ConstitutionConstitution and human rights principles? It is certain that the ban on gatherings in churches and otherplaces of worship is aimed at a higher interest: public health. The practice of religion remainedpossible at home or at a distance, through masses or televised preaching.

The Constitutional Court ruled that the cited executive order was in accordance with the Constitution."[199]. In its decision R.Const.1.200 of April 13, 2020, the Constitutional Court ruled on the state of

---

[195] UN Commission on Human Rights, Siracusa Principles on the Limitation or Derogation Provisions in the International Covenant on Civil and Political Rights, September 28, 1984, E/CN.4/1985/4.
[196] Article 8 ICCPR
[197] UN Human Rights Committee, Freedom of Movement (Art. 12), General Comment No. 27, 1999, § 14.
[198] Article 61 of the Constitution of February 18, 2006...
[199] R. CONST 1,200

emergency and state of siege regime, upon referral for assessment of the conformity with the ConstitutionConstitution of the executive order proclaiming a state of health emergency to deal with the Covid 19 crisis. Articles 61, 85, 119, 144, and 145 determine the powers of each institution: the President, the National Assembly and Senate, Congress, and theConstitutional Court.

Clearly, the state of emergency is legitimate, in accordance with national law, necessary, proportional to the problem to be contained.

The human rights-based approach to treatment and vaccines

Scope and challenges of a rights-based approach

The human rights-based approach is a basic framework on the norms and standards contained in international, regional, and national human rights instruments. It is a growing international consensus on the inclusion of aid within the legal framework of internationally recognized human rights obligations. Reflecting the common position of UN agencies since 2003, this approach builds on the universal framework of international human rights standards on the one hand and recognizes the realization of human rights as a means and an end to development on the other.[200].

On balance, "a human rights-based approach to development means that development is explicitly based on the framework of international human rights law; this involves policies and practices that seek to strengthen the participation and capacities of all those involved in the development process, consistent with human rights. it also invoves, policies and practices that support the right of beneficiaries to active, free, and meaningful participation; addresses discrimination in all its forms prohibited by human rights standards

---

[200] The human rights-based approach to development cooperation - Towards a common position of UN agencies. There is substantial literature on the issue in Bärd A. ANDREASSEN and Stephen P. MARKS (ed), Development as a human right. Legal, political, and economic dimensions, Cambridge, Harvard University Press, 2006; see also Henry J. STEINER, P. ALSTON, R. GOODMAN, International human rights in context. Law, politics, morals. Text and materials, Oxford, Oxford University Press, 2008, pp.1433-1440; the UN approach to the rights-based approach online at www.unescobkk.org/fileadmin/user_upload/appeal/human_rights/UN_Co mmon_understandding_RBA.pdf

and prioritizes those groups most at risk of having their rights violated; holds development processes and its actors accountable to human rights, clearly defining rights and obligations, as well as those who enjoy these rights and those who are required to enforce them.[201].

Such an approach leaves the dynamic of charity, which has long characterized development cooperation, to strengthen the capacities of the poor to demand their rights and of partners to assume their responsibilities.[202]

According to the United Nations, "the adoption of a human rights-based approach ensures that human rights standards, as defined in international law, are used as criteria for guiding policies and addressing specific issues in specific areas. This approach establishes a normative basis that is binding on countries and thus requires legislative intervention at the domestic level. This rights-based approach implies that the beneficiaries of development are active subjects and holders of rights and that duties or obligations are incumbent on those to whom these rights can be enforced (objects or duty bearers)[203]. It has the advantage of being based on both moral consensus and legal obligation, whereas the human development approach, despite its laudable objectives, does not impose specific obligations on individuals, communities, or social institutions either to achieve human development or to ensure its realization at any level, in this or that component.[204].

---

[201] Human Rights-Based Approaches and European Union Development Aid Policies, 2008, 8

[202] Bruno SIMMA, Jo Beatrix ASCHENBRENNER, and Constanze SCHULTEYE, "Human Rights Observations on the European Community's Development Cooperation Activities", in P; ALSTON (ed), The European Union and Human Rights, Brussels, Bruylant, 2001, p. 626.

[203] United Nations, "Coordination of the policies and activities of the specialized agencies and other organizations of the United Nations system in the following area: Coordinated follow-up to and implementation of the Vienna Declaration and Program of Action. Report of the Secretary-General", E/1998/60, June 1, 1998, p. 5.

[204] UNDP, Human Development Report 2000, Human Rights and Human Development, p. 5, Cfr hdr.undp.org/en/media/HDR_2000_ch1_EN.pdf (August 10 2012).

Such an approach emphasizes the responsibility of power-holders: aggrieved rights-holders have the right to sue for redress when the government or other power-holders fail to comply with human rights instruments. Donors should support programs that contribute to the implementation of human rights in the partner country and ensure that no human rights violations occur in the context of the projects carried out. Today, the human rights-based approach commands broad support from the donor community. Over the years, the initial concern with human rights as a conditionality of aid has shifted to donor interventions to support partner countries (and resource-limited countries in particular) to improve respect for human rights[205]. According to Sano, the added value of the rights-based approach is that it strengthens the link between local and global human rights actions, reinforces national advocacy practices, as well as the social and political movements behind them, and proposes a clearer, rights-based definition of the responsibility of governments and non-governmental actors, and stronger protection of the social and civil rights of poor individuals and groups[206].

The approach takes the policies of existing donors and volumes as data and then seeks to achieve human rights within those policies. There is not enough emphasis on the human rights obligations of donors in the aid relationship, nor is there much criticism of aid as an insufficient response to the negative impact of donor trade and foreign policy decisions on the enjoyment of human rights in developing countries. The assertion of states' extraterritorial human rights obligations is not meaningless.

A rights-based approach to Covid-19

The International Covenant on Economic, Social, and Cultural Rights

---

[205]A policy of conditionality means that the extent to which respect for human rights is demonstrated determines the nature and extent of assistance to a specific partner. Conditionality is therefore always distinguished from human rights programs, i.e. reserving part of the available means for the development of programs or projects specifically targeting human rights
[206] H.-O. Sano, "Does Human Rights-based Development make a Difference?" in M. Salamon, A. Tostensen, W. Vandenhole. (Eds.) (2007), Casting the Net Wider: Human Rights, Development and New Duty-Bearers. Antwerp: Intersentia, 78

116

refs to realizing economic, social, and cultural rights through international assistance and cooperation. The ESCR Committee argues that in accordance with Articles 55 and 56 of the UN Charter, with well-established principles of international law, and with the provisions of the Covenant itself, international cooperation for development and thus for the realization of economic, social, and cultural rights, is an obligation of all countries. It is particularly incumbent on countries that are in a position to assist others in this regard[207]. Even acting collectively within an international organization, the extraterritorial responsibility of countries requires that "governments use their influence to ensure that the programs and policies in which they participate do not result in violations of economic, social and cultural rights."[208]. And at the extreme, such a responsibility implies respecting (refraining from violating), protecting (preventing), and fulfilling (through positive measures of realization) the rights at stake. This is where the value of combining efforts to implement the right to health, access to treatment, and access to HIV vaccines becomes apparent. The WHO should remain the focal point for the coordination of various aspects.

At the national level, citizens are equal and enjoy the same rights as human beings; they participate freely and universally in political life and receive or should receive from the country an adequate level of well-being.[209]. The globalization of the economy and of political aspects such as human rights have clearly revealed the end of territories.[210]. "Capital, goods, and people move with such speed and complexity that it is now difficult to make predictions in advance[211]. But if this planetary movement can generate wealth and well-being for the populations, misery is sometimes the result. " Think about the millions of people who pushed to the margins of the economy, are silently sinking into poverty or the cruel scenes of countries torn apart

---

[207] UN Committee on Economic, Social and Cultural Rights, "General Comment No. 3: The nature of States parties' obligations", UN Doc. E/1991/23, para. 14

[208]Maastricht Guidelines on Violations of Economic, Social and Cultural Rights (1997).

[209] UNRISD, State of Disarray. The social impact of globalization, Geneva, 1995, p.xxi

[210] B. BADIE, The end of territories

[211] UNRISD, p.ix

by war[212].

The humanitarian dimension of the crisis does not prevail; vaccines remain protected intellectual property, goods in trade under the WTO. The South African and Indian attempt to get them out of this mercantilist world at the Davos summit was unsuccessful. The WHO, undermined by Trumpism, is trying to mobilize through Covax so that the poor can have access to vaccines. Cuba's health diplomacy, which mobilizes doctors and health workers, could perhaps temper the pharmaceutical industry's drive for "soulless" profit.

But how far can the possible intervention of the WHO be demanded? Is it a right to a vaccine or treatment or pure charity? Is the human rights-based approach so strongly supported by UNagencies feasible in this context? We will have to wait for the coming months and the outcome of the crisis to assess this. However, the pandemic reveals that the world is going through disasters.[213] and (environmental) insecurities that require normative solutions beyond the state sphere, especially for failing states, which cannot solve their problems alone and which need external intervention, whether or not they request it[214]. From the intervention of humanity to theresponsibility to protect!

The fight against the coronavirus pandemic, both nationally and internationally, really demonstrates that poverty is a human rights challenge[215]. In the Congo of the slums and villages, social distancing is difficult to apply because of difficult access to water and hygiene, but also housing in a questionable environment[216]. While the rich have access to high-level hospital facilities, the poor struggle to access poorly equipped health centers in cities such as Kinshasa.
In international relations, vaccination is not posited as a right, im-

---

[212] Ibid
[213] I. STINGERS, In times of disasters. Resist the barbarism that is coming, The impediments to think in circles, 2009, 2005 P.
[214] S.SUR, " On failed states ", The Revue des reviews of the Ministry of Foreign Affairs (France), 2006, www.diplomatie.gouv.fr/fr.
[215] E.DECAUX, A. YOTOPOULOS-MARANGOPOULOS, Poverty, a challenge for human rights, Pais, Pédone, 2009
[216] SUNDI MBAMBI, R. HAMMONDS, The human right to safe water and sanitation in the rural Bas-Fleuve region of the Democratic Republic of Congo: exploring the local conceptions of human rights, Antwerp, 2017

plying equal access and non-discrimination. We have seen Africa being proposed as a testing ground for vaccine research. How can a vaccine be tested on a continent but access to it be so difficult? "Extreme poverty is the main structural and underlying cause of discrimination in the world (...). When you are poor, the doors of access to all human rights seem closed or become inaccessible...a negative proof of the indivisibility of human rights."[217] There is a direct relationship between poverty and health, and the first influences the second.

Indeed, it is true that "the greatest enemy of health in the developing countries is poverty."[218]. Poverty prevents good health management, which leads to poverty. "Illness can reduce household savings and productivity and lead to a diminished quality of life, which creates or perpetuates poverty. The poor, in turn, are exposed to higher personal and environmental risks,are fed less satisfactorily, and have difficulties accessing medical care[219]. In the context of a health emergency or curfew, households making their living in informal economic activities are even more vulnerable as restricted freedom of movement prevents access to resources. Lockdown is detrimental to the health and lives of poor people. A human rights-based approach can circumvent indirect discrimination and cascading rights violations.

Conclusion

"Given the scale of the Covid-19 crisis, the Congolese government should consider notonly the health of each citizen but also all their rights...develop, with its localand international partners, strategies to assist the most vulnerable populations and ensure that health professionals can do their work safely.[220]

---

[217] R. DE GOUTTES, " Double discrimination or cumulative discrimination in access to human rights: the United Nations approach to the problem, "in E. DECAUX, A. YOTOPOULOS-MARANGOPOULOS, op. cit.
[218] K. ANNAN, In Larger Freedom. Development, Security and Human Rights for All, Report, 2001, p. 1
[219] A. BREDIMA, " Right to health and extreme poverty: problems and prospects of a right of questionable effectiveness ", E. DECAUX, A. YOTOPOULOS-MARANGOPOULOS, op. cit, p. 136
[220] Hrw.org/en/news/2020/04/03/rd-Congo...accessed on January 27, 2021, at 08: 42

International cooperation in the fight against poverty and humanitarian emergencies is based on the premise that "poverty, wherever it exists, is a danger to the prosperity of all"[221]. This applies to the Covid-19 pandemic. International solidarity is imperative in the face of the evidence of its globality and its progress, which hardly considers the territorial limits of countries. The internationalization of the fight against major diseases (AIDS, tuberculosis, malaria, SARS, Ebola virus, etc.) should serve as a model for the fight against Covid-19. The issue is also the use of vaccines and essential medicines produced by pharmaceutical companies that aim to make a profit. New medicines are patented and protected at national and international levels. The protection of intellectual property rights should contribute to the promotion of new technology and the dissemination of technology for the mutual benefit of producers and users of technological knowledge (art.7). countries implementing the TRIPS Agreement may adopt measures necessary for the protection of public health. Governments should provide limited exceptions to the exclusive rights protected by the patent. Such exceptions do not unreasonably conflict with patent exploitation and do not prejudice the owner's legitimate interests. This possibility will be advantageous for developing countries, especially in the production of vaccines against HIV.

In this context, a human rights approach could mitigate intellectual property protection, which affects the practice of high prices for medicines that are difficult to access for the poor.[222] people. The ICESCR Committee develops this: core obligations about the right to health include: a) safeguarding the right to health facilities, goods, and services on a non-discriminatory basis, especially about non-vulnerable and marginal groups, and b) the provision of essential medicines, as defined periodically by the WHO Action Program on Essential Medicines[223]. It would mitigate the effects of the rights war.

---

[221] Declaration of the International Labour Conference in Philadelphia in 1944.
[222] A. CHAPMAN, "The human right implication of intellectual property protection", Journal of International Economic Law, 2002, pp.877 et seq
[223] Committee on Economic, Social and Cultural Rights, General Comment No. 14, 2000, UN. Doc (E/C, 12/2000/4)

Ingram Content Group UK Ltd.
Milton Keynes UK
UKHW020702020523
421098UK00014B/374

9 781922 617323